One-Day Retreats
for Junior High Youth

One-Day Retreats
for Junior High Youth

Geri Braden-Whartenby and
Joan Finn Connelly

Saint Mary's Press
Christian Brothers Publications
Winona, Minnesota

To our families, for sharing the gifts of love and spirituality with us, and to the staff of Xavier Retreat and Conference Center, for believing in us, encouraging us, and supporting us.

Authors' Acknowledgments

We wish to thank the Sisters of Charity of Convent Station for having a vision of retreat ministry and a dedication to it. We especially thank Sister Carol Heller, SC, director of Xavier Retreat and Conference Center, for giving us the encouragement and freedom to create the retreats. We are most grateful for her confidence in us and the gift she has for drawing out the best in people. We also thank Marianne Kehoe, program director, for sharing her ideas and for allowing us to use her as a sounding board for our concepts and activities. Thanks to Margaret Clark for proofreading our work. Thanks to all the staff members of Xavier Center who make working there a joy and a privilege.

Thanks also to the thousands of teens who have come on retreat with us and shared their faith with us. This certainly has kept us motivated.

And we wish to thank the adults, both professionals and volunteers, who work with teens. The adults' dedication to the teens and to fostering the teens' faith development have been inspiring for us.

 Genuine recycled paper with 10% post-consumer waste. Printed with soy-based ink.

The cross design on the cover is by Robert Palladino. Used with permission of Printery House of Conception Abbey, Conception, Missouri.

The acknowledgments continue on page 123.

The publishing team for this book included Robert P. Stamschror, development editor; Rebecca Fairbank, copy editor; Barbara Bartelson, production editor and typesetter; Kent Linder, cover designer; Maurine R. Twait, art director; pre-press, printing, and binding by the graphics division of Saint Mary's Press.

Printed in the United States of America

Printing: 9 8 7 6 5 4 3 2 1

Year: 2005 04 03 02 01 00 99 98 97

ISBN 0-88489-436-3

Contents

Introduction

Who We Are

Let us introduce ourselves. We are Geri Braden-Whartenby and Joan Finn Connelly. Each of us is Roman Catholic with a master's degree in religious education from La Salle University, Philadelphia, and a graduate certificate in youth ministry. Geri has been a parish youth minister, a campus minister, and a parish director of religious education. She is now the director of youth services for Xavier Retreat and Conference Center in Convent Station, New Jersey. Joan has been a parish youth minister and a high school religion teacher. She is now the associate youth retreat director at Xavier Center. We each have fourteen years' experience. Together we direct over one hundred retreats a year, and we also do retreat training, and communication and conflict resolution training for adults and teens.

Our Kind of Retreat

Our retreat philosophy incorporates active-learning exercises, a sound biblical foundation, and meaningful prayer experiences. Evaluations returned to us by adult moderators of youth groups have affirmed our philosophy.

Active learning simply means "learning by doing." In our retreats we hope to reach our objectives by having teens use their senses in a variety of ways. Active learning keeps young teens moving, knowing that they will remember much more of what they do than what they hear. A study cited in a 1995 issue of *Group* magazine reports that we remember 20 percent of what we read, 30 percent of what we hear, 40 percent of what we see, 50 percent of what we say, 60 percent of what we do, and 90 percent of what we see, hear, say, and do (p. 16).

Active learning is not all fun and games. It takes more preparation than a lecture and requires more faith and trust because the adult is not controlling the learning by feeding information, but instead is allowing the Holy Spirit to work, through the activities, in the teens themselves. With active learning you are never quite sure of the results. But if it is done well, active learning provides valuable lessons more effectively than does a more rote style of learning.

The Bible is filled with stories of active-learning experiences, each requiring trust that learners would "catch on"—for example, the stories of Abraham and Isaac, Jonah, and Noah and the flood. In Jesus we have a great teacher to follow because he used active learning strategies throughout his life. The storm on the lake, the woman caught in adultery, and the washing of the disciples' feet are examples. It was a pretty risky teaching style, but if God can risk active learning, maybe we can too.

Another part of our retreat philosophy is providing teens with a strong biblical foundation. Each retreat incorporates time for reflection on the Scriptures. Retreatants have the opportunity to read a passage from the Scriptures, reflect on its meaning, and see how the lessons from the passage connect with their personal growth and faith journey. Providing teens with a strong biblical foundation fosters a more mature faith formation.

Each retreat begins and ends with prayer. The opening prayer sets the tone for the day. It creates an environment that encourages teens to be open to God's spirit at work in them. The concluding prayer, a guided meditation, allows teens to listen to God, something that tends to be neglected in their fast-paced lives.

Retreat Overview

Theme

The theme provides the retreat director with a concise purpose for the day.

Bible Basis

The Scripture cite for the message that the combined retreat activities intend to communicate is provided. The Scripture passage both supports the theme of the retreat and serves as the inspiration for creating and selecting the retreat activities. It is also hoped that the teens will come away from the retreat with an appreciation for the richness and guidance the Scriptures provide for their daily life.

Objectives

The objectives expand on the theme and provide specific learning outcomes for the retreat.

Retreat at a Glance

This chart is offered at the beginning of each retreat plan. It gives the director an overview of the retreat, including the time frames and materials needed for each activity.

Retreat in Detail

This section of the retreat plan contains the bulk of the retreat resources. It gives detailed directions for carrying out the activities of the retreat that are listed in the Retreat at a Glance chart. The retreats vary in length but typically run about six hours, and never exceed seven hours. All the retreats include the following elements:

Welcome and Introduction

A spirit of hospitality is conveyed to the teens in the welcome and introduction. If the retreat director does not know the group, this is a good time to start building a rapport with them. In this introduction the retreat director may do one or more of the following tasks:

- Convey appreciation to the teens for taking the time to participate in the retreat.

- Share a personal story from a retreat experience and explain how it affected him or her.
- Explain the significance of a retreat. For example, we tell teens that a retreat is time away from their normal routine to reflect on their life, experience new things, quiet themselves down to be open to God's spirit, pray, enjoy being with their friends, and learn about others.
- Highlight the philosophy of a retreat.
- Communicate the housekeeping information and rules. For example:
  ○ Give directions to the bathrooms and other facilities.
  ○ Explain regulations regarding smoking.
  ○ Offer an explanation of what rooms in the building are available for their use and what areas outside are designated for recreation at lunchtime.
- Go over the retreat theme and schedule. Retreats are not intended to be mystery games. Informing the teens of the retreat theme and schedule demonstrates respect. Most teens are open to whatever you have planned.

   On occasion we have led retreats in which after going over the theme and schedule, the teens said they had already done some of the planned exercises. Sometimes they wanted to do them again, and sometimes they preferred to do something different. Giving the teens some say in the retreat prompts a readiness to participate and a willingness to try new experiences.
- Present the retreat standards. Teens usually come to a retreat with a variety of prior retreat experiences and levels of openness. During the greeting convey that the day will be filled with fun and learning, but along with fun comes some rules. (We call them *standards* rather than rules because teens often have a negative reaction to the word *rules*.) These standards try to anticipate the usual things some teens will do to try to disrupt the retreat (thus heading them off at the pass).

   Standards that we recommended include:
  ○ What's said here, stays here.
  ○ Only one person speaks at a time.
  ○ Put-downs, both verbal and physical, are off-limits.
  ○ Questions are welcomed.
  ○ You may decline when invited to share.
  ○ Be open and try.

   Establishing standards right away gives structure and boundaries to the teens. The boundaries allow them to see that "anything does *not* go" on this retreat. Some young people come because they have to and therefore may express some resentment and resistance. Some come expecting not to participate. The standards clarify acceptable and unacceptable behavior during the retreat.

   After going over the standards, ask the participants if they would like to add any standards to make the day go smoothly. Then direct them to nod if they find the standards reasonable and are willing to abide by them. Post the standards in a place where they can serve as a reminder during the retreat of what the group has agreed on.

Holding the teens accountable to the standards is important. If a standard is violated, acknowledge the violation and its consequences, and remind the young people that they agreed to follow the standards. If this is not done, the standards will not mean anything to the retreatants.

Icebreakers

Icebreakers are important. Part A of the appendix offers several to choose from, or you can use your own. Icebreakers conducted at the beginning of the retreat are meant to help relax the young people, show them that the retreat is meant to be fun as well as spiritual, and get them accustomed to working in small groups. Icebreakers conducted immediately following lunch are meant to bridge the transition between the unstructured lunchtime and the structured program. These games help the teens refocus and re-enter the spirit of the retreat.

The following guidelines will help to enhance the effectiveness of icebreakers:

- Practice them ahead of time to ensure you have all the necessary materials and are able to give clear directions.
- Have some large-group icebreakers and then some small-group ones.
- Do not use icebreakers that might embarrass some retreatants.
- Do not continue to play the games over and over. They are meant to be introductory.
- Do not be afraid to try the same icebreaker again with a new group if the first group did not like it or if it did not go well the first time. For example, we often start our retreats with the icebreaker People Upset (see part A of the appendix). It is a great large-group game that gets teens running around and intermingling. The game involves different people winding up as leader in the center of the circle. We played the game with a group we did not know well, and one teen stood in the center of the circle. We waited for him to make the next move, but he did not. A teacher quickly came over and told us that the young man was a new resident of the United States and did not speak English. We respectfully invited him back to the group and assigned another teen to continue the game. If that had been our first experience with People Upset, we may never have used it again. Not all icebreakers work with all groups. If one occasionally does not work, it may not be the icebreaker but the makeup of the group.

Opening Prayer

Simple opening prayers are provided for each retreat. They may be read aloud by the teens or by the retreat director. You may want to add a song, or you may want to allow time for individual petitions, knowing that "where two or three are gathered in Christ's name, there he is."

Retreat Activities

A variety of activities flesh out each retreat. These include personal reflection exercises and small- and large-group activities. You may wish to keep the same small groups throughout the retreat or to form new groups for each small-group activity. That is up to you. All the instructions needed to carry out the activities are included. Each activity builds on the previous one. The retreats usually start with light, simple activities. As the day progresses, the activities become more challenging. Therefore, we encourage you to use the activities in the order presented.

Affirmation

Going through adolescence is a tough experience. Teens need to know that they are loved for who they are and who they are becoming. Statistics show that from sixth grade to twelfth grade a young person's self-image typically decreases. There are many reasons for this: media portrayals of the ideal person, biological changes going on inside the teenager, attraction to the other sex, and the added stress of more responsibility.

Unfortunately teens focus on negative images of themselves rather than on positive ones. To compensate for this, affirmation is built in throughout the retreats, and one specific affirmation activity is placed near the end of each retreat so that the teens can leave with positive feelings.

Closing Guided Meditation

Many teens have told us that they really like guided meditations. They say that these experiences provide some of the few opportunities they have to relax and really pray. After one guided meditation, a young man said that he really liked it. When asked why, he responded, "My father has been dead awhile, and during the meditation I got to speak with him one more time."

Concluding each retreat with a guided meditation not only gives teens this quiet time to be with God but also shows them that God is truly present in their life.

Progressive Muscle Relaxation

Starting a guided meditation with progressive muscle relaxation allows the teens to calm themselves down enough to be open to the guided meditation. Several progressive muscle relaxation exercises are given in part C of the appendix.

Evaluation

Evaluation helps teens reflect on the whole retreat and what it has meant to them. A simple way to do this is to ask these three questions:
• If you had only one word to describe today, what one word would you pick?

- What is one new thing you learned today, or what is one thing that you really liked?
- What do you feel God is challenging you to do as a result of this retreat?

Helpful Hints

We have found the following strategies to be useful in making the retreat run smoothly:

- When teens are in small groups working on an assignment, alert them to the time remaining with 5-minute, 2-minute, and 1-minute signals. This helps them pace themselves so that they will not be surprised or upset when time is called.
- In some of the retreat activities, we assign teens to be leaders by calling out a certain quality or criterion, such as, "those whose birthday is closest to Christmas," or "the person with the longest name." A variety of measures like these increases the likelihood that during the retreat many young people will have the opportunity to be a leader.
- During break time the retreatants may choose to eat a snack. We inform them before they take their break to finish all food or drink before returning to the meeting area. Having teens eating and drinking during the retreat activities is not only distracting for them but for the retreat director as well.
- Be prepared. Gather all needed materials before the retreat. If the retreat director appears unprepared, the teens will know it. Time spent finding things disrupts the flow of the retreat and loses the teens' attention.
- The material in this book is geared for groups of up to thirty-five participants, with the whole group often being separated into small groups. The ideal small-group size is six to eight participants. Because significant small-group activity is part of the retreat, we encourage you to used trained small-group facilitators. Trained facilitators will enhance the retreat experience for the teens. (See part D of the appendix for a list of tips you can provide to facilitators.) Facilitators can be older high school students, teachers, parents, catechists, or other volunteers. Facilitators are especially helpful for younger teens who may or may not be used to working together.

Debriefing Activities

Most of the retreat activities end with questions that can be used to discuss the meaning of that particular exercise. As alternatives to posing the questions to the large group and having volunteers answer, you could do the following:

- Have the teens return to their small groups and discuss the questions. Then invite each small-group leader to report back to the large group.
- Assign different questions to each small group and have the small-group leaders report back to the large group.

- Decide as a group on a one-sentence moral to the exercise. Present the moral or message in a creative fashion, such as a song, a bumper sticker, or a mime.

Competition Versus Cooperation

The directions for some of our icebreakers and retreat activities suggest telling the group that the first team finished "wins." We certainly want teens to feel good about themselves throughout the retreat, and not to be put in the position of being "losers." However, teens in the United States are used to competing, and many are motivated by rewards. The icebreakers and some of the small-group activities that appear to be competitive in nature actually challenge the teens to cooperate as a team within small groups and to engage only in mini-competition with other small groups.

We give prizes to winning teams only when doing so is necessary to the activity. When prizes are not required, we tell winning teams who ask what their reward or prize is, "You win our deepest appreciation and congratulations." At the end of each game or performance-type activity, we applaud those who participated.

Some groups need to be motivated initially by some form of competition. If you feel that your group does not need the added motivation that competition provides, simply give instructions for the groups to accomplish the activity, and call time when they appear to be finished.

We usually remark at some point in the retreat that we enjoyed many games that did not involve declaring a winner. We try to help the young people realize that participating in an activity and working cooperatively with their team members is more important than winning.

Our Hope

Retreats have proven to be valuable and effective in the faith formation of teens. We hope that the retreats in this book prove to be an effective tool to help bring your group to a deeper faith.

Retreat 1

Christian Community

Theme This retreat shows teens why it is important to be a part of a Christian community and how they can create and participate actively in one.

Bible Basis *1 Cor. 12:12–27.* Jesus reminds us how important each of us is by comparing our various gifts and talents to the parts of the body.

Objectives The retreatants will do the following:
- examine how being a member of a secular community is different from being a member of a Christian community
- reflect on why it's important to be an active member of a Christian community
- recognize cooperation as an asset to a Christian community
- assess and affirm their personal gifts and talents, building on the values recorded by Paul in 1 Cor. 12:12–27

Retreat at a Glance

The following chart offers a brief overview of the retreat activities, time frames, and materials needed. For more detailed information about any of the activities, refer to the directions given in the Retreat in Detail section.

ACTIVITY	TIME FRAME	SUPPLIES
Welcome and Introduction	10–15 minutes	poster with standards
Icebreakers	15–30 minutes	depends on selection
Opening Prayer	5 minutes	Bible
Human Machine Building	20–30 minutes	
Community	10 minutes	newsprint, markers,
The Giving Cycle	10 minutes	candy or other playing pieces
Christian Community	10–15 minutes	newsprint, markers
Put-Ups and Put-Downs	15 minutes	pencils, paper, newsprint, markers
Don't Stomp on Me	10 minutes	empty soda cans, board or carpet square
Break	10 minutes	
Draw It Together	20 minutes	resource 1–A, pencils, blank paper
Scripture Reflection	10 minutes	
The Body of Christ	20–30 minutes	handout 1-A, pencils
Lunch	45 minutes	
Icebreakers	15 minutes	depends on selection
Yes, No, Maybe	15 minutes	
Community Acrostic	15–20 minutes	newsprint, markers
What Are You Made Of?	15–20 minutes	markers or crayons, paper
Yarn Closing	15–20 minutes	large ball of yarn
Closing Guided Meditation	20–30 minutes	instrumental music, tape or CD player
Evaluation	5 minutes	pencils, paper

Retreat in Detail

Welcome and Introduction (10–15 minutes)

Icebreakers (15–30 minutes)
Choose from among the icebreakers offered in part A of the appendix of this book, or use games of your own.

Opening Prayer (5 minutes)
Begin the prayer by reading 1 Cor. 12:12,18–19,25–27, which is Paul's description of us as the Body of Christ. Then share the following prayer in your own words:
• Dear God, thank you for making each one of us unique and special. Continue to encourage us to use our gifts to help one another. Remind us when we put others down that we all are made in your image and are important. Guide us in building up our world into a community unified in your love. Amen.

Human Machine Building Small-Group Activity (20–30 minutes)
This activity encourages the teens to reflect on their ability to cooperate and participate in a community.

1. Form the teens into small groups. Each small group will make itself into a machine that others will likely recognize. Begin by demonstrating a "human machine," for example, a washing machine. You will need three volunteers. Direct two volunteers to form the washing machine tub and the third person to be the agitator. Direct the two volunteers representing the tub to hold hands, with the agitator standing inside the circle. Instruct the agitator to twirl around when the signal to begin is given. When the three volunteers have finished demonstrating the machine, invite the rest of the retreatants to guess what machine was acted out.

2. After someone successfully guesses washing machine, continue by saying something like this:
• Now it is your turn as small groups to create a human machine. As you begin, consider the following questions:
  ◦ What machine do you want to build?
  ◦ Is it possible to create the machine with your small group?
  ◦ What are the parts of this machine?
  ◦ Which part do you want to be? Everyone must play one part of the machine.
  ◦ Is the machine complete?
  Take time to practice. You may use sounds.
  Give the small groups time to practice. If other rooms in the building are available for your use, assign a separate area to each group so that the groups may practice privately. Call them back after 10 minutes.

3. Before the small groups take turns performing their machine, give the following directions:

• After each small group finishes performing its machine, the rest of the groups should try to guess what it is. It is okay if two groups perform the same machine because each small group will likely present the machine in a unique way.

Call for a group to volunteer to go first. Applaud after each small group has performed its machine.

4. To conclude the activity, lead a discussion with the whole group using the following questions (see the introduction for alternative ways of debriefing this and other retreat activities):

• How did your group decide what machine it would be?
• What made this exercise easy or difficult?
• What was your biggest obstacle? Why?
• How did you get over this obstacle? How did your team feel as it overcame obstacles?
• Was it easy or difficult to work with the other members of your small group? Why? What did you learn from working together?
• What does this exercise tell us about community?

Community

Large-Group Brainstorming (10 minutes)
On a sheet of newsprint, write the word *community*. Invite the retreatants to call out words and images that come to mind when they hear this term. This brainstorming helps the retreatants to see the various components of the many communities to which they belong.

After the large group has finished brainstorming, invite a volunteer to compose a definition of the word *community* based on the words and images listed on the newsprint. Make sure the rest of the group agrees to the definition and then write it on the newsprint. Leave the definition up for the duration of the retreat. The teens will compare this definition with the definition of *Christian community*, which they will compose in an upcoming activity.

The Giving Cycle

Large-Group Activity (10 minutes)
The purpose of this exercise is for the young people to experience giving and receiving.

Begin by directing the teens to form a circle with their chairs. Then give each person three pieces of the same item: for example, candy, pennies, or poker chips. (If candy is used, inform the teens not to eat any. Each person will be allowed to eat one piece at the end of the game.)

Explain the rules this way:

• This game has only two simple rules: First, if someone offers you a piece of candy, you must take it. Second, you must give away all your candy, one piece at a time. When I give the signal to begin, you may stand up and move around the inside of the circle. You will have 3 minutes to give away your candy. When I call time, sit down and wait for the next instructions.

Some teens may ask what the goal of the game is or other questions. If that occurs, simply repeat the directions as stated. It is okay if the teens are confused.

At the end of the game, collect the playing pieces. If candy was used, you may want to allow each teen to eat one piece.

Conclude the activity by leading a discussion of the following questions:

- Was it easy or difficult to give away your candy? Why?
- Was it easy or difficult to accept others' candy? Why?
- What feelings did you have? Were you pleased? frustrated? happy? sad?
- Did any of you want to participate less? participate more? Why?
- What would you do differently the next time?
- How does this activity demonstrate belonging or the lack of it?

Supplement the teens' comments by saying that giving and receiving go hand in hand. If all of us concentrate on giving love, each of us will feel overwhelmed with the care we receive, and we will realize that we belong.

Christian Community

Large-Group Brainstorming (10–15 minutes)
This brainstorming enables the group to discern the various components of Christian community.

On newsprint write the phrase *Christian community*. Let the retreatants call out words and images that come to mind when they hear that phrase.

After the group has finished brainstorming, invite a volunteer to compose a definition for the phrase *Christian community* based on the words and images listed on the newsprint. Make sure the rest of the group agrees to the definition and then write it on the newsprint.

Lead a discussion of the following questions:

- What's the main difference between secular communities and Christian communities?
- What are the values that guide each of these types of communities?
- What does a Christian community offer that secular communities do not?
- Does our society live by these Christian qualities and values? Why or why not?
- How can we bring Christian values and qualities into our society?

Put-Ups and Put-Downs

Small-Group Activity (15 minutes)
This activity encourages the retreatants to reflect on the power of language.

Begin by directing the teens to form small groups. Explain the activity in your own words as follows:

- For this exercise your group will need a recorder and a reporter. The recorder writes down the group's answers. And, after all the small groups are finished discussing and writing, the reporter reads the group's findings aloud to everyone. Let's have the recorder be the person in your group with the shortest hair, and the reporter, the person with the longest hair.

  Make a vertical line down the center of a piece of paper. On the top left side, write "Put-Downs," and on the top right side, write "Put-Ups." Think of times when people have said things to you that were really "downers"—comments that made you feel bad. Put-downs can be angry comments, insults, or criticisms. Write these in the "Put-Downs" column. Then think of times when people have said things to you that were "uppers"—that made you feel good. Put these comments in the "Put-Ups" column. As a small group you are to list as many put-downs and put-ups that you can recall others saying.

After a few minutes, call time and express the following in your own words:

- Now I want you to think of times when *you* said a put-down or put-up to someone else. Add these to your list.

Next, direct the reporters to count up the number of put-downs and put-ups and report both numbers to the large group. Record the numerical results on newsprint. Chances are there will be more put-downs than put-ups.

Ask these questions:

- Why is it easier to come up with more put-downs than put-ups?
- What attitudes toward others do we need in order to use more put-ups?

Don't Stomp on Me

Large-Group Activity (10 minutes)

This exercise helps the young people reflect on how crushing put-downs can be.

Have a good supply of clean, empty soda cans available. Place on the floor a board or carpet square on which the cans can be crushed.

Direct the reporters from the previous exercise to come up to the front of the room and take turns sharing with the large group several (three to five) put-ups their group listed and then three put-downs. After sharing his or her group's put-downs, direct each reporter to stomp on and crush a soda can.

Conclude the activity with a discussion of the following questions:

- Who can restore the soda can to its original shape?
- Why can't anyone restore the can to its original shape?
- What does this exercise teach us about put-downs?
- Which is easier to restore—someone's self-esteem after it has been stomped on, or this can after it has been crushed? Why?
- What does it take to restore someone's self-esteem?
- What are the negative results of using put-downs?

Break

(10 minutes)

Draw It Together

Small-Group Activity (20 minutes)

This activity highlights the value of each person in a community.

Form teams of four members. Assign each member of each team a different one of the following body parts: eyes, ears, feet, or hands. Give the teens designated as the hands a piece of blank paper and a pencil. Separate the team members, putting the hands in a different room if possible. Give the teens designated as the eyes a copy of resource 1–A, "Draw It Together Diagrams." The eyes each describe one of the diagrams on the resource to their teammate who is the ears (without the ears seeing the resource). The ears listen attentively to the description and remember it. Then the ears each describe what they heard to their teammate who is the feet. The feet each go and describe the diagram to their teammate who is the hands. The hands must draw what the feet described. (It's similar to the telephone game.)

Discuss the activity using the following questions:

- How different were the drawings from the original diagrams? Why?
- Who was the most important member of the team?
- How important is clear communication among team members? Why?

Summarize the meaning of the activity in words similar to these:

- This experience is like being part of the church. All of us have different functions, but all of us are so important that the church would be crippled without us.

Scripture Reflection

Large-Group Activity (10 minutes)

In this activity the teens experience the Scriptures in a new way.

Introduce the activity by telling the retreatants they will hear a reading from the Scriptures that has been adapted for group participation.

Then assign equal numbers of people to each of the following parts: hands, ears, eyes, nose, and feet. Give each part an action to perform:

- *Hands.* Clap.
- *Ears.* Say "Eh."
- *Eyes.* Hold up their index finger and say "I."
- *Nose.* Take a deep breath in.
- *Feet.* Stomp on the floor.

Give the following directions and then deliver the reading, pausing at the ellipses (. . .):

- Whenever I say the word *one,* everyone should stand up in their place and then sit down immediately. When I name your assigned body part, perform your assigned action. Thus, during the reading you will be moving or making sounds whenever you hear the word *one* or your body part. This is a reading adapted from First Corinthians, chapter 12:

The body is a unity, though it is made up of many members. Though its parts are many, they form *one* . . . body. So it is with Christ. For we were all baptized by *one* . . . Spirit into *one* . . . body. Now the body is not made up of *one* . . . part, but of many.

If the *foot* . . . should say, "Because I am not an *eye,* . . . I don't belong to the body," that would be downright silly. If the whole body were an *eye,* . . . where would the *ears* . . . and the sense of hearing be? But if the whole body were an *ear,* . . . where would the *nose* . . . and the sense of smell be?

God has arranged the parts of the body just as God wanted them to be. If they were all *one* . . . part, where would the body be? As it is, there are many parts, but *one* . . . body. The *eye* . . . can't say to the *hand* . . . "I don't need you." And the *nose* . . . can't say to the *feet* . . . "I don't need you." For God doesn't want the body parts to argue, but to care for one another equally. That way if *one* . . . part is honored, every part rejoices with it.

Summarize the meaning of the activity in your own words:
- Just as it took everyone's participation to make this Scripture passage come alive, so, too, it takes everyone sharing their abilities and gifts to make a community come alive and stay dynamic.

The Body of Christ

Small-Group Activity (20–30 minutes)

This activity fosters in the teens an understanding of, and appreciation for, the variety of God-given gifts and talents that each teen possesses.

1. Direct the retreatants to form small groups. Give each person a copy of handout 1–A, "The Body of Christ." Then offer the following instructions:
- First read over the entire handout. Then put your initials on the line in front of the parts you feel describe you best; pick your three strongest talents. Then look at the other people in your small group and decide which part best describes each person. Put each person's initials on the line in front of the part you believe best describes her or him.

2. After everyone has completed the handout, say something like this:
- The person with the birthday closest to today's date will begin by explaining what he or she selected for himself or herself. Then the other small-group members will explain what they wrote down for the person who just spoke. The teen who was spoken about then may comment on the other members' selections. It's okay if everyone comes up with different qualities, because the way we see ourselves is not always the way others see us. Repeat the procedure until each member of your group has been spoken about.

3. After the groups are finished, lead a large-group discussion of the following questions:
- Were the parts you chose for yourself the same as the parts others chose for you? Why or why not?
- Pretend someone in your group behaved like one of the body-part descriptions on the handout. How would that person feel? How would others treat him or her?
- The parts of the body contribute to the whole. In what ways do the individuals in your group contribute to the functioning of the group as a whole? In what ways do you contribute?
- How do you feel when a member refuses to contribute? when a member is not allowed to contribute?

Lunch

(45 minutes)

Icebreakers

(15 minutes)

Choose from among the icebreakers offered in part A of the appendix of this book, or use games of your own.

Yes, No, Maybe

Large-Group Activity (15 minutes)

This activity challenges the teens to articulate what they believe about God and the Christian community. The exercise is meant to stimulate discussion, encouraging the teens to think and share their various opinions. It is not meant to be a test. Unless a teen is extremely wrong, do not correct him or her. This may be difficult to do, but keep in mind that your role is one of facilitator, not teacher. Just keep challenging the teens to defend their position. Use questions like these: How have you come to believe that? What would make you change your mind? What makes it so hard to believe . . . ?

Direct the students to sit in chairs in a circle. Then give the following introduction in your own words:

- I am going to read a statement. If you agree with the statement, stand up in front of your chair. If you disagree, sit on the floor in front of your chair. If you are not sure whether you agree or disagree, remain seated in your chair.

After reading each of the statements below, direct the teens to make their choice. Then call for volunteers to explain why they agree, disagree, or are unsure about the statement.

- Most people in my church say they are Christians, but they really are not Christians.
- Being a member of a Christian community means that I cannot do all the fun things my friends do.
- You can tell whether a person is a Christian by the way he or she acts.
- Christians love everyone.
- If there were fewer hypocrites in church, more people would want to attend.
- The church has little or no impact on today's society.
- Watching a Mass on television is just as good as attending one.
- Smaller churches are better than big ones.
- If your church is boring, you should change churches.
- It's important to choose friends who believe the same things about God as you do.
- A family can be a Christian community.
- There's more to being a member of a Christian community than going to church once a week.
- In a Christian community it's easy to share my gifts and talents.
- The most important community to belong to is the Christian community.
- Service to others is an important value in our society.
- If a person doubts God or doubts what the Bible says, she or he can still be a Christian.
- The main advantage to being a Christian is going to heaven.
- I want the faith of the church to be passed on to the next generation. [Say this one last.]

Community Acrostic

Small-Group Activity (15–20 minutes)

In this activity the retreatants brainstorm tangible strategies and ideas that teens can use to help build community in their school, church, and neighborhood.

Direct the teens to form small groups. Give each small group a sheet of newsprint and a marker. Tell half the groups to make an acrostic using the word *build,* and the other half to make an acrostic with the word *community.* Share these directions:

- Take the word that has been assigned to your group, either *build* or *community,* and write that word vertically down the left-hand side of a piece of newsprint. Then, as a small group, brainstorm ideas for building community in your school, church, or neighborhood that begin with each letter of your assigned word. For example [demonstrate on newsprint]:

Become friends with all kinds of people.
U
I
L
D

Compliment others often.
O
M
M
U
N
I
T
Y

When the small groups are finished, invite each one to share its acrostic with the large group.

What Are You Made Of?

Small-Group Activity (15–20 minutes)
In this activity the retreatants reflect on the qualities of a Christian.

Invite the young people to show one another the various labels on their clothing. Ask if anyone has a piece of clothing that is 100 percent of anything (for example, silk, cotton, polyester). Say something like this:

- Today we have discussed what it means to be a Christian and how to use those qualities to build up a Christian community. Just as clothing has many contents, so there are many components to being a Christian. In your small group create a label for a Christian. It could be 50 percent loving and 50 percent giving; or 50 percent loving, 25 percent giving, and 25 percent faithful. You decide on the contents.

After the groups are done, have one person from each group report the group's answer. If time allows, distribute paper and markers or crayons, and direct the groups to create a label for a Christian.

Yarn Closing

Affirmation (15–20 minutes)
The purpose of this activity is twofold: (1) to give everyone an opportunity to publicly give thanks to God for one of their gifts or talents and (2) to create a yarn web to illustrate the interdependence of gifts in a community.

1. Direct the teens to sit in a big circle on the floor. With a large ball of yarn in your hands, give the following instruction:

• Think about how you would complete the following statement: "I can contribute to my community because God gave me the gift of . . ."

After giving the teens time to think, describe the following procedure:

• After each person completes the statement, he or she holds on to a piece of the yarn and tosses the ball to someone on the opposite side of the circle. That person then completes the statement, holds on to the piece of yarn, and tosses the ball to someone else. We will continue until everyone has had a turn.

Some teens may complete the statement by saying, "my family" or "life." These are beautiful statements, but the purpose of the activity is for the teens to share a personal gift or talent. If a teen says "my family" or "life," ask him or her to share a specific gift or talent. Also, some teens may be embarrassed by this activity and thus say that they cannot think of an answer. If that happens, invite other teens or adults to say aloud the various gifts or talents this person possesses. Then have the person choose one of those gifts to complete the statement.

2. When all have finished completing the statement and have a hold on the yarn, ask the following questions:

• What have we created here?
• What does this image illustrate about being part of a Christian community?
• What might the yarn represent and why?
• What is this yarn doing for us physically?

3. Next, invite two or three teens to let go of the yarn and then ask:

• What happened when some people let go of the yarn? Why?
• What does this say about Christian community?

Closing Guided Meditation

(20–30 minutes)

Begin the meditation with a progressive muscle relaxation exercise (see part C of the appendix for suggestions). If possible, play soft instrumental background music. Then continue with the following guided meditation. Pause for a few seconds at each ellipsis (. . .).

• Sometimes we feel a part of a group, and other times we feel rejected and alone. Jesus understands that and reminds us that he is our best friend and is always with us, especially in difficult times.

Imagine that you wake up on the heaven highway by yourself. . . . The highway stretches as far as you can see. . . . Nothing else is around. . . . It's a peaceful place, but a little lonely. . . . Suddenly from afar you see a car on this highway headed in your direction. . . . The car pulls up next to you, and a bunch of people start to get out so that you won't be alone. . . . First Saint Peter comes out. He calls you by name, but he doesn't look like the saint from the Bible. . . . He's young like you and dresses a little like you, too. . . . He has a big smile on his face, says hi, and offers you a cool drink. . . . Next, out comes Saint John, and he offers you a piece of your favorite candy. . . . Then out comes the Virgin Mary, and she asks how everything is going. . . . Next, out come two other saints. . . . They are all laughing, patting you on the back, and saying how much they want you to be a part of their group. . . .

One more person is still in the car. He slowly begins to get out. . . . As this person makes his way through the crowd of your new friends, you recognize him as Jesus. . . . He has a big smile on his face that shows how much he loves you. . . . You're overwhelmed by his love and how great you feel that so many saints are with you and are your friends. . . . You're overwhelmed by Jesus' unconditional love. . . . You know from those eyes that he will always love you, does not judge you, and constantly calls you to be your best. . . .

Jesus says, "Why don't we go for a short walk where we can talk?" . . . You walk a little way on the heaven highway and stop in front of a bench. . . . Jesus invites you to sit on the bench and talk with him. He has some questions for you, and he would like you to ask him some questions as well. . . .

Jesus says: "My disciples are my closest friends. They are my family. Is there anything you would like me to do for your friends and family?" Spend some time sharing with Jesus. [Longer pause.]

Jesus goes on to say: "Being part of a community requires commitment. What's holding you back from being more committed to your church and to me?" [Longer pause.]

Jesus remarks: "You are very special. God has given you many gifts that our world needs. What are some talents you recently shared that helped another person?" [Longer pause.]

Jesus has one more question for you: "What's the hardest part of being a Christian, and how can I help you?" [Longer pause.]

Jesus asks if you have any questions for him. Spend a few minutes, if you would like, asking Jesus some questions and listening to his responses. [Longer pause.]

Jesus says: "I have a gift for you—the gift of friendship, my friendship. . . . No matter where you go or who you meet or who you leave, you will always have me. . . . I want to be your best friend and spend time with you. . . . So anytime you want to get together, quiet yourself and call my name, and I will come to you. . . . I love you very much. You do not need to fear."

Jesus explains that he's really enjoyed this time together, but he must go now. He stands up from the bench and begins to walk down the heaven highway. . . . As he walks further and further away, he appears smaller and smaller. . . . Now you no longer can see him, but you still feel his presence and friendship. . . . You close your eyes for a moment and say a little prayer of gratitude for your best friend, Jesus, and all the things you talked about with him: "Jesus, thank you for always being there for me. Help me to see my part in the Body of Christ and to always believe in myself and in you. Amen."

When you open your eyes, you will no longer be sitting on the bench on the heaven highway, but back here in this room. When you are ready, slowly open your eyes and come back.

Evaluation

Large Group (5 minutes)

After the guided meditation, direct the teens to reflect in writing on the following questions. Invite them to answer aloud if they feel comfortable doing so.

- If you had only one word to describe today, what word would you pick?
- What is one new thing you learned today, or what is one thing you really liked? (It could be something we did or something someone said.)
- What do you feel God is challenging you to do as a result of this retreat?

Draw It Together Diagrams

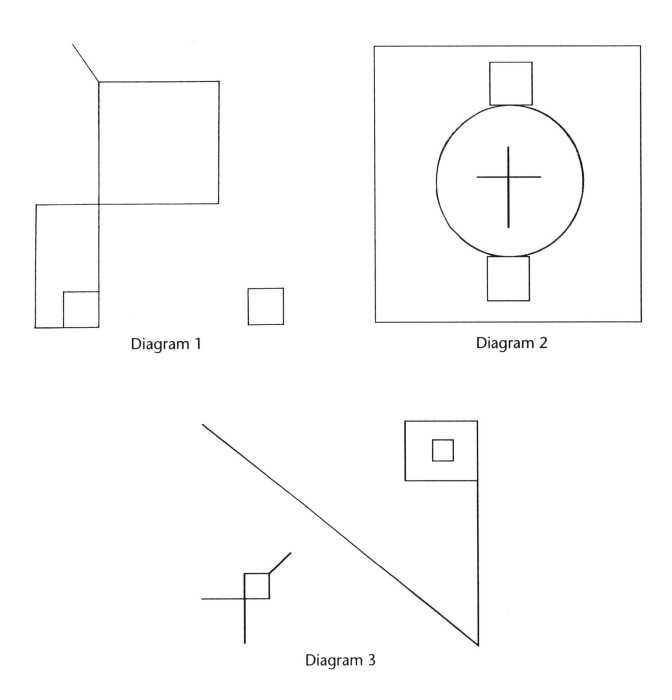

Diagram 1

Diagram 2

Diagram 3

The Body of Christ

The drawing below represents our church. Write your initials on the line next to the three parts of the body that best describe you and the unique talents and gifts you share with the church.

Next, write in the initials of each member of your small group next to the body part that you believe best describes her or him.

_____ _____ *Head.* Smart, teaches others

_____ _____ *Ears.* Listens well

_____ _____ *Funny bone.* Makes people laugh, has a good sense of humor

_____ _____ *Backbone.* Has a lot of courage

_____ _____ *Eyes.* Always watches out for others

_____ _____ *Mouth.* Has good things to say, articulates well

_____ _____ *Shoulders.* Supports and helps other people

_____ _____ *Heart.* Is caring and loving

_____ _____ *Fingers.* Is good at building things

_____ _____ *Hands.* Is creative and artistic

_____ _____ *Legs.* Is athletic and strong

_____ _____ *Knees.* Prays and has a deep faith

Retreat 2

Freshman Survival

Theme This retreat offers teens tips and strategies for coping successfully with the major changes they will experience during their first year of high school.

Bible Basis *Gen. 12:1–9.* In the story of Abram, we can relate to someone who had to make a major transition in his life and learn how to cope with the resulting changes.

Objectives The retreatants will do the following:
- explore the benefits and value of new experiences
- express their hopes and fears about becoming freshmen
- learn positive ways of coping with loneliness
- develop strategies to reduce stress

Retreat at a Glance

The following chart offers a brief overview of the retreat activities, time frames, and materials needed. For more detailed information about any of the activities, refer to the directions given in the Retreat in Detail section.

Note: Prior to the retreat, photocopy and assemble into booklets the set of handouts for this retreat. Make a booklet for each retreatant. See page 41 for further instructions on preparing the booklets.

ACTIVITY	TIME FRAME	SUPPLIES
Welcome and Introduction	10–15 minutes	poster with standards
Icebreakers	15–30 minutes	depends on selection
Opening Prayer	5 minutes	Bible
Write Right	5 minutes	handout booklets, pencils
New Home	15–20 minutes	Bible, booklets, pencils, newsprint, markers
Survival Game	25–30 minutes	booklets, pencils
Physical Mathematics	10–15 minutes	
Self-Profile	20–30 minutes	booklets, pencils
Break	10 minutes	
Loneliness Easers	20 minutes	Bible, envelopes with loneliness easers, glue, booklets
Everybody's Afraid Sometimes	15–20 minutes	Bibles
Survival Tips for Freshmen	10–15 minutes	booklets
Lunch	45 minutes	
Icebreakers	15 minutes	depends on selection
Follow the Leader	10–15 minutes	
Pinned	15 minutes	clothespins
Sandy's Stress	20–25 minutes	a yoke with buckets, rope, stones, newsprint, markers, booklets, pencils
Amazing Prophecies	15 minutes	booklets, pencils
Closing Guided Meditation	20–30 minutes	instrumental music, tape or CD player
Evaluation	5 minutes	pencils, paper

Retreat in Detail

Welcome and Introduction
(10–15 minutes)

Icebreakers
(15–30 minutes)
Choose from among the icebreakers offered in the appendix of this book, or use games of your own.

Opening Prayer
(5 minutes)
Begin by reading Gen. 12:1–2,4—the story of Abram. Finish by sharing the following prayer in your own words:
• Dear God, just as you appointed and supported Abram to travel to a foreign land and do your work, so too have you appointed us. Just as Abram was afraid of new adventures, so too are we sometimes wary of changes in our life. Yet, like Abram, we are excited about maturing, growing, and facing new challenges.

We are moving away from familiar things, from some friends we have known for many years. Just as you promised Abram that you would always be with him—to encourage and protect him—so too be with us. Thank you for creating us and guiding us. Thank you for always being with us. Amen.

Write Right
Large-Group Activity (5 minutes)
In this activity the participants experience the awkwardness of change.

Begin by distributing the handout booklets and having the teens sign their name on the cover as legibly as possible using the hand they usually do not write with.

Lead a large-group discussion based on the following questions (see the introduction for alternative ways of debriefing this and other retreat activities):
• How did you feel during this activity?
• Could you write with the opposite hand regularly if necessary?
• What would it take for you to become accustomed to writing with your opposite hand?

Summarize the meaning of the activity in the following way:
• Sometimes change is hard, but we usually find the strength to adapt and deal with it. Today we will talk about changes in our lives—especially school-related changes.

(Adapted from Margaret Hinchey, "Back-to-School Changes," *Jr. High Ministry*, August–September 1992, p. 34. Reprinted by permission from *Jr. High Ministry* Magazine, copyright © 1992 by Group Publishing, P.O. Box 481, Loveland, CO 80539.)

New Home
Small-Group Activity (15–20 minutes)
In this activity the teens explore a Scripture passage that exemplifies how one faith-filled person trusted in God during a time of transition.

1. Have one volunteer read aloud Gen. 12:1–9. Encourage reflection on the Scripture passage by asking this question:

- Why would we focus on this Bible passage when we are talking about changes in our life?

2. Continue by offering these directions in your own words:
- In Abram's day it was unusual for people to move more than a few miles away from home. So Abram's change took courage. God gave him the courage to make the change.

   Now open your booklet to page 1. Under the heading "Abram," list the changes or unusual challenges you think Abram and his family faced as they traveled to a new home.

   Under the heading "Me," list the changes or unusual challenges you think you will face when you go to high school.

3. When the teens are finished writing their lists, have them form small groups. Give each small group a sheet of newsprint and a marker. Explain the activity in your own words:
- Now everyone is to share their list with the other members of their small group. Each small group will need a recorder and a reporter. The recorder writes down the group's answers on a sheet of news-print, and after the groups are finished discussing and writing, the reporter reads the group's answers aloud. Let the oldest person in your group be the recorder, and the youngest one, the reporter.

   When the groups are finished writing and discussing, invite the reporters up to the front of the room and have them share their group's list.

4. Summarize the activity this way:
- By reflecting on this passage from Genesis, we can see that many similarities exist between your situation and Abram's. Going through change is not always easy. The one thing that sustained Abram was his trust in God. You are invited to do the same.

(Adapted from Hinchey, "Back-to-School Changes," p. 35. Reprinted by permission from *Jr. High Ministry* Magazine, copyright © 1992 by Group Publishing, P.O. Box 481, Loveland, CO 80539.)

The Survival Game

Small-Group Activity (25–30 minutes)
This activity helps the retreatants learn that establishing priorities sometimes calls us to make difficult choices.

1. Begin by asking the whole group what they think the word *survival* means and why this retreat is called "Freshman Survival." Then have the retreatants form small groups. Give them these instructions:
- We are going to do a little exercise in survival. Pretend that an impending catastrophic disaster is expected to occur in the very near future, so that life as we know it in the United States may come to an end. You have been chosen to be part of a select group of persons who is going to travel to a remote place in order to start a new community and continue civilization.

   Open your booklet to page 2. Listed there are some things you would like to take with you. You are not sure you will be able to take everything. So in case you have to leave something behind, you need to rank these things in the order of their importance. Make 1 your highest priority, and 12, your lowest.

Give everyone a few minutes individually to rank the items.

2. Continue with words similar to these:
• Now your small group has to decide which items you would take if you were the group selected to survive. The group can take only nine of the twelve items. This time the tallest person in your group will serve as the recorder, and the shortest will be the reporter.

   After the groups have spent 5 to 10 minutes deciding what to select, interrupt them with an "emergency message" that states they can now take only seven items. Give them a few more minutes to narrow their selections. Then invite the reporter from each group to share its list.

3. To conclude the activity, lead a discussion with the whole group using the following questions:
• Are your Christian values reflected by your top choices?
• What are some things we take for granted in our everyday lives?
• What are some things for which you are thankful to God? How can you express your thankfulness?
• What does this exercise say about individual survival and group survival?
   (Adapted from Griggs, *Twenty New Ways of Teaching the Bible*, p. 27)

Physical Mathematics

Small-Group Activity (10–15 minutes)

This lighthearted activity provides a break for the teens. It comes in between two reflective activities.

   Give the small groups these instructions:
• I will ask you a series of mathematical questions. After each question, your group is to arrange themselves on the floor to form the numerical answer. The first small group to form themselves into the correct answer scores one point.
   ○ The total number of times your team members have brushed their pearly white teeth today.
   ○ The total number of years your team has been alive.
   ○ The number of days of the flood recorded in Genesis minus the number of days in January. [9]
   ○ The number of Gospels multiplied by the number of times Jesus changed water into wine. [4]
   ○ The number of Christ's Apostles minus the number of months in a year. [0]
   ○ The number of commandments given to Moses minus the number of days of Creation. [3]
   ○ The number of times Jesus tells Peter to forgive his brother in Matthew 18:22, minus forty times the number of tribes in Israel. [10]

(Adapted from Thomas Iwanowski, "Try This One: Physical Mathematics," *Group Inside*, October 1992, p. 59. Reprinted by permission from *Group* Magazine, copyright © 1992 by Group Publishing, P.O. Box 481, Loveland, CO 80539.)

Self-Profile

Small-Group Activity (20–30 minutes)

This activity allows the teens to express their concerns and fears about moving on to high school.

1. Instruct the small groups to turn to page 3 in their handout booklet. Give them 10 minutes to complete the survey by themselves. Then call time and continue with these instructions:
   - Now you will have an opportunity to share your answers with the members of your small group. This time the leader for your group will be the person with the longest last name. The leader's role is to share his or her response to the first question and to ask the other members of the small group to share their answers and explain why they answered the way they did. Continue sharing responses and explanations until time is called.

2. Call time after 10 minutes and lead a discussion with the whole group based on the following questions:
   - Did you discover anything new about yourself while doing the survey?
   - What are some things that may help a person "survive" freshman year?
   - Why is it important to discuss the statements and questions on the survey?

   This would be an appropriate time for you as the retreat director to share a personal story about your freshman year.

3. In conclusion convey these ideas in your own words:
   - We all have to survive things every day. Some are minor and some are major events—from surviving a test to surviving the loss of a person or pet. We can learn survival skills to help us cope. One way we survive well is by sharing with other people our fears and our concerns. God sent Jesus down in the form of a human person to remind us of that. God is very close to us. When we share, sometimes our fears and concerns don't seem so big anymore.

Break

(10 minutes)

Loneliness Easers

Small-Group Activity (20 minutes)

This activity is intended to expose the teens to healthy ways of dealing with lonely times in their lives.

1. Begin by asking the whole group what they think the difference is between being alone and being lonely. After eliciting their responses, say something like the following:
   - You're vulnerable when you're lonely. The word *vulnerable* means "prone to injury."

     Invite a volunteer to read Deut. 30:19–20. Then ask:
   - What are some harmful quick fixes people may use when they are lonely?

Offer a response like the following to the young people's answers:

- Some people may use alcohol or sex to block the pain of loneliness. But these "solutions" don't really address the problem. They make us feel better for a while, but then we wake up feeling guilty or hurt, or suffering from a hangover. What responses to loneliness might lead to real solutions rather than temporary ones?

2. Give each teen an envelope containing a set of loneliness easers from handout 2–F, "Loneliness Easer Strategies." Have the teens sit on the floor and arrange the loneliness easers in front of them in order from those they are most likely to use to those they are least likely to use. After they rank the loneliness easers, direct them to glue them in priority order onto page 4 of their booklet.

3. When all have completed the task, direct the teens to return to their small group. Give the following instructions:
- This time the small-group leader will be the person in each group with the smallest shoe size. The leader is to ask the following questions of her or his group and then report back to the large group.
   ○ Which loneliness easer did you rank number 1? Why?
   ○ Which loneliness easer did you rank the lowest? In what situations might a person use this strategy?
   ○ Which loneliness easer can you start using now?
   Call time after approximately 10 minutes. Invite the small-group leaders to share the significant points from their discussions. (As an alternative to gluing the easers in their booklet, the teens could make ladders out of dowels and Popsicle sticks and glue the easers on the rungs in the order in which they use them.)
   (Adapted from Dockrey, *Jr. High Retreats and Lock-Ins,* pp. 161–162)

Everybody's Afraid Sometimes

Small-Group Scripture Activity (15–20 minutes)

The purpose of this activity is to identify individuals from the Scriptures who, despite their fears, placed their trust in God.

1. Introduce the activity this way:
- We are going to find out how other people have dealt with times when they were feeling lonely and afraid, and see if we can learn something from their experience. Your small group will have a person from the Scriptures to read about. Then your small group must come up with a creative mime to tell the story of your assigned person. The other small groups will try to guess which person from the Scriptures you are presenting.
   Assign each small group one of the following passages:
- *Matt. 26:36–45.* Jesus in Gethsemane
- *Luke 1:26–38.* The Virgin Mary and the angel Gabriel
- *Exod. 3:1–12.* Moses and the burning bush
- *Acts 9:1–9.* Saint Paul knocked from his horse
- *Jonah 1:1–17.* Jonah and the whale
- *Matt. 14:1–31.* Saint Peter walking on water
- *1 Sam. 17: 4–7,10,32–37,48–50.* David and Goliath
- *Matt. 28:1–10.* Mary Magdalene at the tomb
Give the small groups enough time to prepare their mime.

2. Call each small group to the front of the room one at a time to present its mime. After each small group's presentation, applaud and then ask the members of the presenting group the following questions:
• What was this person feeling? Why?
• What helped this person overcome this feeling?

3. Wrap up this activity by repeating some of the groups' answers to the last question. If trusting in God was not listed, this is a good time to remind the teens that trusting in God will give them the strength to overcome their fears.

Survival Tips for Freshmen

Large-Group Activity (10–15 minutes)
This activity presents the teens with practical suggestions for getting through freshman year.

Ask the teens to arrange their chairs in one large circle. Direct them to open their booklet to page 5, "Survival Tips for Freshmen." Call for volunteers to read the tips aloud.

Conclude the activity by leading a discussion of the following questions:
• Which tip do you see as most important for you right now?
• Can you think of other tips to add to our list?
• Are there any tips you disagree with? Why?

Lunch
(45 minutes)

Icebreakers
(15 minutes)
Choose from among the icebreakers offered in the appendix of this book, or use games of your own.

Follow the Leader

Large-Group Activity (10–15 minutes)
This activity gets the teens thinking about the qualities of a leader in an amusing way.

Form one large circle with the teens sitting in chairs. Ask one volunteer to leave the room. Choose one person in the circle to be the leader. Have this person lead actions for others to follow, such as clapping hands, snapping fingers, and patting legs. Encourage the leader to change actions frequently and discreetly so that the volunteer will have a hard time guessing who's the leader.

Direct the leader to start performing an action. Call the volunteer back into the room. Have the volunteer stand in the center of the circle. Give the volunteer three chances to guess who the leader is. Play this game two more times with two new volunteers.

Highlight the qualities of a leader by asking these questions:
• Think of some leaders in your school. What do you admire about them?
• What things do they do well?
• What are the qualities of a competent leader?
• How can you use these leadership qualities during your freshman year?
(Adapted from Cindy Hansen, "Ready-to-Go Meetings: Cheers for Peers," *Group,* February 1992, p. 54. Reprinted by permission from *Group* Magazine, copyright © 1992 by Group Publishing, P.O. Box 481, Loveland, CO 80539.)

Pinned   Large-Group Activity (15 minutes)

This activity engages the teens in a game in which competition may tempt them to cheat.

Give each teen five clothespins. Instruct the teens using words similar to the following:

- On "Go," you are to move around the room and clip one clothespin at a time to someone else's clothes. You may pin only one on at a time. When you have pinned all your clothespins, remove clothespins from your clothes one at a time and pin them on someone else.

  Do not block someone else from pinning a clothespin on you. You may move out of the way, but using your hands to block someone from pinning you is against the rules. No running and no talking are allowed during the game. When I call time, stop where you are.

  During the game, do not enforce the rules. After 4 minutes, call time. Ask the teens to count their clothespins. Then tell the teens to line up according to the number of clothespins they have—on their clothes and in their hands.

  Continue the activity by asking the following questions of the whole group:

- Did you like this game? Why or why not?
- If you were not doing well, were you tempted to cheat? Explain.
- What were some ways people might have cheated?
- What might motivate someone to cheat?
- What might motivate someone to avoid the temptation to cheat?
- How is this game similar to other situations in which people are tempted?

  Conclude the activity by saying something like the following:

- Cheating is one temptation we know many teens may experience in high school. The next activity looks at some other temptations you may be confronted with.

(Adapted from "It's So Tempting," *Jr. High Ministry,*
March–April 1991, p. 30. Reprinted by
permission from *Jr. High Ministry* Magazine, copyright © 1991 by
Group Publishing, P.O. Box 481, Loveland, CO 80539.)

Sandy's Stress   Large-Group Activity (20–25 minutes)

In this activity the retreatants identify possible stresses they may face freshman year, and brainstorm suggestions that will help them reduce or avoid such stresses.

Before the retreat, make a yoke out of a piece of wood, with a bucket hanging by a rope from each side.

1. Assemble the large group. Call for a volunteer to wear the yoke, explaining that at certain points during the story, stones will be placed in the buckets, weighing the person down. (If making a yoke is not possible, you can stack books or bricks on the volunteer's wrists and outstretched arms instead.) Invite a second volunteer to put the stones in the buckets when directed to do so.

Read the following story aloud to the large group. Pause at each asterisk (*) and have the second volunteer burden the person with the yoke by placing a stone in each bucket.

- This is the story of Sandy and her first day of high school. Sandy was very excited and nervous about attending high school, but that didn't stop her from having fun the night before. She figured her carefree summer life was swiftly coming to an end, so she spent the night before her first day of high school with some of her friends. They stayed out later than they should have, and Sandy was very tired. *

  As things happen, when Sandy finally looked over at her alarm clock, it read 7:30 a.m. "Oh no," she shouted, "I set that for 6:30! Why didn't it go off like it was supposed to?" * She quickly jumped out of bed, took a shower, and dressed. As she was putting on her shoes, the shoelace broke. "Oh well," she thought, "no time to get a new one now. I'll just have to hobble my way through classes today." *

  Fortunately Sandy did not miss her bus. "That would have been the last straw," she thought. When she got on the bus, she found a seat and looked around. "These don't look like my classmates," she observed. When she asked the bus driver about it, she found out she had gotten on the wrong bus. * Fortunately the high school was not that far from the bus's destination, and if she ran, she could make it to school on time. *

  Sandy rushed as much as she could, but she still walked into her first class five minutes late and was sent to the office for a demerit. "I can't get a break," she reflected. * The rest of the morning actually went smoothly. Sandy met up with many of her old friends and talked and made friends with new people.

  When lunch came, Sandy spotted some of her friends and went to sit with them. By the time she got there, all the seats were taken. After looking all over the cafeteria for a chair, she realized she had only ten minutes left for lunch. * When she reached into her purse, she discovered she had left her wallet at home. "I don't have time to eat anyway," she lamented. * One of her friends offered her some food, which made her feel better.

  After lunch Sandy stopped off at the bathroom. This was a place filled with much activity. Upper-class students were there selling answers to quizzes and exams, and some had drugs that they offered to Sandy. * They assured Sandy that everyone did drugs, and no one would be caught. * Sandy was feeling so tired, hungry, and lonely at this point that she almost gave in.

2. Remove the yoke from the volunteer. Process the activity with the whole group using the following questions:
- What were the various stresses Sandy encountered?
- How did Sandy feel?

3. Reread the story, pausing at each * to invite the group to share things Sandy could have done to avoid or ease that stress. Write these suggestions on newsprint. Next, direct the teens to open their handout booklet to page 6, "What Sandy Could Have Done." Have the teens copy the suggestions from the newsprint into their booklet.

4. Conclude the activity with words similar to these:
- Although Sandy's first day of high school was filled with more stress than you will probably encounter, her story can teach you ways to avoid or reduce stress when it happens to you. Having a list of suggestions to choose from will help you when you encounter stress.

Amazing Prophecies

Affirmation (15 minutes)

In this activity the teens affirm one another for the special qualities they have, and imagine ways these qualities will help them in the future.

Instruct the teens to turn to the back cover of their booklet, titled "Amazing Prophecies." Say something like this:
- Each one of us has been blessed by God with many gifts and talents. Sometimes others see things in us that we don't see in ourselves. This is your opportunity to tell your peers what you admire most about them and what good things you believe the future holds for them. Write your name in the middle of the page. When I give the signal to begin, put your booklet, with your name facing up, on your chair. Then go to any chair you choose, read the name, and write a talent or quality you appreciate about that person and a prophecy or prediction you have about his or her future. For example, you have a great talent for writing. I see you winning the Nobel Prize for literature. Do not sign your name; this is meant to be anonymous. This activity is an affirmation—a time to compliment others. Please do not joke around. If you really can't write something nice in a person's booklet, then don't write anything.

Give the signal "Go" to begin the activity. Allow enough time for the teens to write in as many booklets as they choose. Make sure that at least one affirmation is written in everyone's booklet. Call time to end the activity and invite the teens to go back to their chair and read their affirmations.

Direct the teens to each pick the statement written on their booklet that they appreciate most. Invite them to share aloud that one statement.

Closing Guided Meditation

(20–30 minutes)

Begin the meditation with a progressive muscle relaxation exercise (see part C of the appendix for suggestions). If possible, play soft instrumental background music. Then continue with the following guided meditation. Pause for a few seconds at each ellipsis (. . .).
- Change can be exciting as well as scary. People in the Hebrew Scriptures, like Abram and Sarah, were called to trust God in all things. They sought God's help in times of need, and rejoiced and thanked God for the good things that happened to them. God was with Abram and Sarah, and God continues to be with each one of us today—right now.

Imagine yourself on a deserted island. . . . On one side of you is the ocean as far as you can see. . . . On the other side are trees and flowers. . . . You're feeling a little scared because you've never been here before, but also peaceful because everything around you is beautiful. . . . The flowers are all different colors, and when a breeze comes by, you can smell the sweetness of the plants. . . .

In front of you, through the trees, is a path. . . . You're not sure if you should take it. . . . It would be wonderful to see if there are other people on this island, yet there could be wild animals or harmful plants. . . .

While you're still deciding whether you should stay here by the shore or venture onto the path, you suddenly see someone coming through the trees. . . . Instantly you know it's Jesus. . . . You feel relieved now that he's here. . . . As Jesus walks closer to you, you notice how peaceful he is, how loving his eyes are, and how joyful his smile is. . . .

Now Jesus is right next to you. He says "Hello." . . . He invites you to sit down on the beach with him for a while to talk. . . .

Jesus asks you, "What are some of your fears about freshman year?" . . . Spend some time talking with Jesus. [Longer pause.]

Jesus continues, "What do you think you will need to do to overcome some of those fears?" [Longer pause.]

Jesus says: "When I was on earth, there were times I was afraid. It was then that I would quiet myself down and pray. . . . God gave me the courage to face new challenges. God will give you the courage to do new things, too."

Jesus adds: "Let's overcome the fear you have of walking on that path by walking it together." . . . The two of you stand up and start walking toward the path, away from the beach. . . . Before you were afraid to go, but with Jesus by your side, you're feeling adventurous and excited. . . .

Now you're inside what seems to be a forest. . . . It's cooler in here. . . . As you walk, Jesus asks, "What are some of your talents or traits that you are really proud of?" [Longer pause.]

Jesus continues, "I'm very proud of you for trying something new by coming with me into the forest." . . .

Now you've reached the end of the path. . . . In front of you is a bench in a small clearing. . . . The two of you walk over to the bench and sit down. . . . The sun is bright and warms you. . . . Jesus asks, "What are some of your dreams, your goals for your future?" [Longer pause.]

Jesus reminds you that just as he is here with you right now, he will be with you as you work toward your goals. . . . He asks if there's anything else you'd like to talk to him about before he leaves. Spend this time talking with Jesus and listening to him. [Longer pause.]

Jesus needs to leave now and reminds you that whenever you want to talk again, he will be there. . . . Jesus gets up, gives you a handshake, looks into your eyes, and tells you how much he loves you and that he is always with you. . . . You feel very confident and peaceful. . . .

Now Jesus turns and walks back onto the path and into the trees. . . . You can no longer see him. . . . Now you close your eyes and say a prayer: "Jesus, thank you for reminding me that you have always been with me and will continue to support me, guide me, listen to me, and encourage me. Let me look forward to new adventures, even when I feel scared. It's okay to be afraid, and it's okay to let go of my fears and trust in you. You are a special gift to me. I am so very lucky. Amen."

When you open your eyes, you will no longer be on the bench but back here in this room. When you're ready, slowly open your eyes and come back.

Evaluation

Large Group (5 minutes)

After the guided meditation, direct the teens to reflect in writing on the following questions. Invite them to answer aloud if they feel comfortable doing so.

- If you had only one word to describe today, what word would you pick?
- What is one new thing you learned today, or what is one thing you really liked? (It could be something we did or something someone said.)
- What do you feel God is challenging you to do as a result of this retreat?

Handout Booklet

The handouts for this retreat get made into a handout booklet. This is accomplished by photocopying the handouts so that they are double-sided and stapling them together. Some of the handouts are provided here; others you create yourself. Directions for each handout follow below.

Handout 2–A. You provide it. It is a sheet for the cover of the booklet containing the title "Freshman Survival Guide." Add an illustration if you wish. This handout is used with the Write Right activity.

Handout 2–B. You provide it. It is a sheet of paper with a vertical line down the middle, forming two columns. The heading for the left-hand column is "Abram," and the heading for the right-hand column is "Me." It is used with the New Home activity. This handout is page 1.

Handout 2–C, "Priorities," is provided here for you to reproduce. It is used with the Survival Game activity. This handout is page 2.

Handout 2–D, "Self-Profile," is provided here for you to reproduce. It is used with the Self-Profile activity. This handout is page 3.

Handout 2–E. You provide it. It is a sheet of paper with the title "Loneliness Easers." It is used with the Loneliness Easers activity. This handout is page 4.

Handout 2–F, "Loneliness Easer Strategies," is provided here for you to reproduce. After making the appropriate number of copies, cut the strips apart on the dashed lines and give each teen a set that she or he will glue to page 4 of the booklet.

Handout 2–G, "Survival Tips for Freshmen," is provided here for you to reproduce. It is used with the Survival Tips for Freshmen activity. This handout is page 5.

Handout 2–H. You provide it. It is a sheet of paper with the title "What Sandy Could Have Done." It is used with the Sandy's Stress activity. This handout is page 6.

Handout 2–I. You provide it. It is a sheet of paper with the title "Amazing Prophecies." It is used with the Amazing Prophecies: Affirmation activity. This handout serves as the back cover of the handout booklet.

Priorities

An impending catastrophic disaster is going to end life as we know it in the United States. You have been chosen to travel to a remote location in order to start a new community. Listed below are some things you would like to take with you, but you may not be able to take everything. Rank the following items from highest to lowest priority, using **1** for the highest and **12** for the lowest.

_____ A variety of fruit and vegetable seeds

_____ A collection of books of poems, novels, biographies, and short stories

_____ Several animals of your choice

_____ A medicine chest with medicines and first-aid equipment

_____ Some basic tools like hammers, saws, shovels, hoes, and axes

_____ A sewing machine, sewing materials, and fabrics

_____ A windmill and electric generator

_____ Some other books like a medical encyclopedia, farming and construction manuals, the Bible, and a dictionary

_____ A battery-operated radio and tape recorder with a collection of fifty selected tape recordings and some blank tapes

_____ Several musical instruments and books of music

_____ A small chest of odds and ends like thread, needles, eating and cooking utensils, candles, ropes, and so on

_____ One other item of your choice. What is it? _____

(Adapted from Donald L. Griggs, _Twenty New Ways of Teaching the Bible_ [Nashville: Abingdon Press, 1979], page 27)

2

Self-Profile

A difficult part about being a freshman will be (circle Y=yes; M=maybe; N=no)

1. Not having all my friends go to my high school		Y M N
2. Being in new surroundings and being unsure where everything is		Y M N
3. Being taken advantage of by upper-class students		Y M N
4. Always having to be cautious so as not to do something stupid and be laughed at or joked about		Y M N
5. The first test in each subject		Y M N
6. Getting used to new teachers		Y M N
7. Other (add your own)_____		Y M N

Deep down inside, I am (place an X on the spot on each spectrum that indicates where you see yourself.)

1. Easygoing——————————————————————Hyper
2. Listener—————————————————————————Talker
3. Leader——————————————————————————Follower
4. Doer——————————————————————————————Thinker
5. Player————————————————————————————Spectator
6. Introvert——————————————————————————Extrovert

Around people I do not know, I am usually (circle two)

a. super cool	**b.** nervous	**c.** quiet	**d.** outgoing
e. goofy	**f.** confident	**g.** cautious	**h.** other _____

In new situations, I usually feel (circle two)

a. tongue-tied	**b.** excited	**c.** awkward	**d.** comfortable
e. painfully shy	**f.** relaxed	**g.** frightened	**h.** other _____

When it comes to making a tough decision, I generally (circle one)

a. struggle for days	**e.** make a snap decision
b. wait to see what someone else decides	**f.** ask for advice
c. hope it will go away	**g.** take a long walk
d. pray	**h.** other _____

(Adapted from Paul Baker, "Freshman Survival Night," *Group,* May 1985, page 58.
Reprinted by permission from *Group* Magazine, copyright © 1995, Group Publishing,
P.O. Box 481, Loveland, CO 80539. Idea for self-profile by Geri Braden-Whartenby.)

3

Handout 2–D: Permission to reproduce this handout for use in your program is granted.

Loneliness Easer Strategies

Cut into strips along the dashed lines. Give each teen one set of strips.

-- ✂ ---

Talk to a friend.

-- ✂ ---

Read the Bible.

-- ✂ ---

Stay by myself for a little while.

-- ✂ ---

Read a good book or magazine.

-- ✂ ---

Listen to an uplifting song.

-- ✂ ---

Invite a friend to do something with me.

-- ✂ ---

Figure out why I'm lonely.

-- ✂ ---

Talk to someone about how I feel.

-- ✂ ---

Write my feelings in a poem, story, journal, or letter.

-- ✂ ---

Concentrate on someone else's problems.

-- ✂ ---

Play a musical instrument.

-- ✂ ---

Find something to do to keep busy.

-- ✂ ---

Other _____

-- ✂ ---

(Adapted from Karen Dockrey, *Jr. High Retreats and Lock-Ins*
[Loveland, CO: Group Books, 1990], page 163)

Survival Tips for Freshmen

1. Exercise—walk, run, or play.

2. Be good to yourself—get some rest; eat a good meal.

3. Celebrate small victories—treat yourself to a banana split when you ace that math test or finish a project.

4. Help someone in need.

5. Write a thank-you note to someone who helped you.

6. Talk to a trusted adult friend outside your family.

7. Watch how you react to others. Don't let them control your feelings.

8. List your fears and worries. Pray about them each day.

9. List the good things in your life and thank God for them.

(Adapted from Ann Cannon, "Making Sense of Moods: Blues-Buster Tips," *Jr. High Ministry*, September–October 1991, page 41. Reprinted by permission from *Jr. High Ministry* Magazine, copyright © 1991 by Group Publishing, P.O. Box 481, Loveland, CO 80539.)

5

Retreat 3

Peacemaking

Theme   What is it that keeps us from being "good Sams" (good Samaritans)? In this retreat the teens explore the problems of prejudice, stereotyping, lack of empathy, and insufficient knowledge.

Bible Basis   *Luke 10:30–37.* In the parable of the good Samaritan, Jesus reminds us that to be peacemakers we must reach out to people in need, even those we find hard to love.

Objectives   The retreatants will do the following:
- define what a peacemaker is
- recognize that Jesus calls us through his teachings and example to be peacemakers
- appreciate that being prejudiced is a roadblock to being a peacemaker
- become aware of the effects of the unequal distribution of resources in our world

Retreat at a Glance

The following chart offers a brief overview of the retreat activities, time frames, and materials needed. For more detailed information about any of the activities, refer to the directions given in the Retreat in Detail section.

ACTIVITY	TIME FRAME	SUPPLIES
Welcome and Introduction	10–15 minutes	poster with standards
Icebreakers	15–30 minutes	depends on selection
Opening Prayer	5 minutes	Bible
Defining *Peace*	10 minutes	newsprint, markers
Peacemaker Balloons	10 minutes	uninflated balloons, small strips of paper, pencils, newsprint, marker
Jesus the Peacemaker	10–15 minutes	Bible
Givens and Changeables	10–15 minutes	poster board, marker, masking tape
Good Sam	20 minutes	slips of paper, pencils, Bible, construction paper, markers
But I Say to You	10–15 minutes	handout 3–A, newsprint, markers, Bibles
Break	10 minutes	
Gilbert and the Color Orange	15–20 minutes	newsprint, markers
The Factory	15 minutes	
Lunch	45 minutes	
Icebreakers	10–15 minutes	depends on selection
World Simulation Game	45 minutes	masking tape, colored construction paper, blindfolds, mouth gags, string, tables, chairs, art supplies (see p. 57), candy, Bible, newsprint, marker
Front Page	15 minutes	resource 3–A, pencils, markers
Spiral of Peace	15–20 minutes	resource 3–B, markers, scissors, hole punchers, string
Closing Guided Meditation	20–30 minutes	instrumental music, tape or CD player
Evaluation	5 minutes	pencils, paper

Retreat in Detail

Welcome and Introduction (10–15 minutes)

Icebreakers (15–30 minutes)

Choose from among the icebreakers offered in part A of the appendix of this book, or use games of your own.

Opening Prayer (5 minutes)

Begin the prayer by reading Luke 10:30–37, the parable of the good Samaritan. Finish with a prayer similar to the following:

- Dear God, we have only to look at the news to realize that our world is not a totally peace-filled place. Even among children and teens there is violence, prejudice, and anger. Lord, help us to be instruments of your peace. Guide us in making our world a place of compassion and healing, rather than a place of division and strife. Give us the courage to be good Samaritans by going out and touching those who are hurt and disadvantaged. May your peace always surround us. Amen.

Defining *Peace:* Large-Group Brainstorming (10 minutes)

Coming up with a group definition of the word *peace* is the goal of this activity.

On a sheet of newsprint, write the word *peace*. Instruct the group by saying something like the following:

- Please call out any words or images that come to your mind when you hear the word *peace*.

Record on the newsprint the words or images the young people offer. After everyone has had a chance to share, conclude the activity by discussing this question:

- We are going to explore our attitudes toward peace. Do you believe that peace is possible? If so, why? If not, why not?

Leave the brainstorming list up for the entire retreat.

Peacemaker Balloons Small-Group Activity (10 minutes)

In this activity small groups unscramble the definition of the word *peacemaker*.

Form the participants into small groups. Give each small group one uninflated balloon, inside of which is fourteen clues on tiny, folded pieces of paper. The clues consist of one word each from this definition: A peacemaker has compassion for others and tries to relieve their pain through action.

Direct the groups to blow up their balloon and tie it. Then have one person in each group volunteer to sit on the balloon until it pops, releasing the fourteen clues. Have the groups try to arrange the words into a definition. Instruct the team that solves the mystery definition first to read it aloud and write it on the newsprint.

Lead a discussion with the whole group based on the following questions (see the introduction for alternative ways of debriefing this and the other retreat activities):
• What does compassion mean?
• What are some of the types of pain in our world today?
• What are some actions people are taking today in their home, school, town, or nation to relieve the pain of others?

Jesus the Peacemaker

Large-Group Activity (10–15 minutes)
This activity highlights Jesus as our role model for peacemaking.

1. Call for two volunteers. Have each read one of the following Scripture passages: Matt. 9:1–8 and Matt. 9:9–13. Then pose the following questions for group discussion:
• Why do you think Jesus acted the way he did?
• What made it easy for Jesus to act this way? What made it difficult?
• How did Jesus treat these people? Why did he treat them that way?
• What did others say about how Jesus acted?
• Who can give me some other examples of times when Jesus was a peacemaker? [Remind them to name times when Jesus showed compassion and, through his actions, relieved another's pain.]
• Why do we call Jesus a peacemaker?

2. Move on by saying something like this:
• God sent Jesus to us to be our role model, to show us how God wants us to act. Just as it was sometimes easy for Jesus to be a peacemaker, it was also sometimes very difficult. The same is true for us.
Continue the discussion by asking the whole group these questions:
• Can anyone describe a time when you or someone you know acted like a peacemaker?
• Was this peacemaker someone in history or someone in your town?
• What made it easy for you or them to be a peacemaker? What made it difficult?

3. Conclude the activity by expressing this idea in your own words:
• During our retreat together we hope to explore ways that we can act like Jesus and be peacemakers, too.

Givens and Changeables

Large-Group Activity (10–15 minutes)
This activity helps the teens begin to distinguish between the elements of their lives and their world that can be changed and those that cannot be changed.

Before the retreat, create two posters: one labeled "Given," and the other, "Changeable." Hang the posters on opposite sides of the room.

1. Begin the activity by communicating these directions:
• In this activity you will be giving your opinion about various elements in our society. If you think an item is a "given," move to the side of the room with the poster labeled "Given." Similarly, move to the other side of the room if you think the item is "changeable." If you are undecided, then stay in the center of the room. Givens cannot and will not be changed; they are absolutely necessary or always present. Changeables are not absolutely necessary and can be changed.

It is likely—and okay—that the retreatants will have a wide range of opinions.

Suggested items for givens and changeables are faith, church, racism, God, school, love, crime, drug abuse, cancer, death, drunk driving, disease, pollution, poverty, world hunger, gender differences, survival of the strongest, war, taxes, homework. Use as many of these items as time allows.

Allow up to 2 minutes of discussion between each item for the retreatants to say why they moved where they did. Again emphasize that people have different ways of seeing the same thing. Invite a couple of people to explain their position. Try to involve different people in the discussion of each item. Do not feel you have to use all the items suggested, and feel free to add some of your own. Stop the activity when the pace begins to slow.

Option. If space is very limited, you might give each person two different colored cards, one for given and one for changeable. Ask the teens to vote by holding up one of the cards.

2. Process the activity with the whole group by asking these questions:
• What things do you think Jesus believes are given? What things does he see as changeable? Why?
• What does society say is given? What is changeable? Why?
• Did you change your mind about any of the items after hearing others' comments?

3. Conclude the activity this way:
• There's a prayer you may have heard before that talks about givens and changeables. It's called the Serenity Prayer:
   ○ God, grant me
        Serenity to accept the things I cannot change,
        Courage to change the things I can, and
        Wisdom to know the difference.
   Ask:
• How can this prayer help with some of the items we talked about?
                (Adapted from Huntly, *Rich World, Poor World,* pp. 277–278)

Good Sam — Large-Group Activity (20 minutes)

The purpose of this activity is to help the retreatants understand, through the use of the parable of the good Samaritan, our responsibility to help other people.

1. Give each teen a piece of paper with one of the following instructions on it:
• Act tough and mean (but not physically violent).
• Ignore anyone who complains.
• Show concern for those who complain or act injured.
• Complain about an injury or lie on the floor as if you are in pain.
Explain these directions to the retreatants:
• Each person's piece of paper identifies a role for her or him to play. When I say "Go," act as the instructions on the paper tell you to. After a few minutes, I will call time and end the game.

Give the group the signal to begin. After a few minutes, call time and have everyone return to their seat. Spark a discussion by asking this question:
• Can you guess which Bible story you have just acted out?

2. After someone guesses correctly, invite a volunteer to read aloud Luke 10:30–37. Then pose these questions to the group:
• Who did you portray in the story?
• How did the character as you portrayed it compare to the character in the parable?
• How did your character feel in the parable?
• How are people today like the priest and the Levite?
• Why was the good Samaritan willing to help the injured man?
• What did the Samaritan receive for his trouble?

3. Form pairs and give each pair a sheet of construction paper and a marker. Direct the pairs to design a business card for the good Samaritan based on how he handled himself.

After completing their project, invite the pairs to take turns sharing their good Samaritan business card.

4. Conclude the activity by raising these questions:
• Would you be able to write your name on this business card? Why or why not?
• As a friend, how are you like or unlike Sam (the good Samaritan)?
• Is Sam a peacemaker?
• What prevents us from being good Sams?
(Adapted from "Ready-to-Go Meetings: Good Samaritan Friendship," *Group*, November–December 1990, pp. 65–66. Reprinted by permission from *Group* Magazine, copyright © 1990 by Group Publishing, P.O. Box 481, Loveland, CO 80539.)

But I Say to You   **Small-Group Activity (10–15 minutes)**
In this activity the retreatants examine popular wisdom and compare it to the wisdom of Jesus.

Form small groups. Distribute to each small group one copy of handout 3–A, "But I Say to You," a sheet of newsprint, a marker, and a Bible.

Begin by expressing the following thoughts in your own words:
• Our society gives us a lot of advice on how to live. The Bible also gives us advice. Oftentimes the two contradict each other. Jesus promises us that if we follow his example and the advice from him and the Scriptures, we will have fulfilled lives. Let's look at some of the advice and wisdom of our society and of God.

Your group will need a recorder—someone to write down your group's answers. You will also need a reporter—someone to read aloud what was decided. Let's have the person in each group with the longest hair be the recorder, and the person with the shortest hair be the reporter. Any questions?

Assign each small group one popular wisdom to work on. Give the groups these instructions:
- Write on your sheet of newsprint a Christian response to the popular wisdom statement you are assigned, referring to the Bible passages cited.

Do one of the listed wisdoms with the whole group as an example of what the teens are to do in their small groups. Here is one example:
- "Take good care of yourself. Watch out for number one."

    Read 2 Cor. 8:8–15. Some Christian responses to this popular wisdom may be:
    ○ God wants everyone to have what they need.
    ○ Do not be afraid to give even if it's hard to do.
    ○ God will take care of you because when you are in need, others will give to you.
    ○ It's more important to give than to receive.
    ○ You will be rewarded for your giving.

    Challenge the teens to come up with as many responses as possible. If you would like, have them create a rap number or jingle for their favorite Christian response.

    After the groups are finished, invite them to post their newsprint and share their responses with the other groups.

    (Adapted from Bright, ed., *Poverty: Do It Justice!* p. 89)

Break (10 minutes)

Gilbert and the Color Orange

Large-Group Activity (15–20 minutes)

This activity helps the retreatants understand the origins and meaning of prejudice.

1. Read the following story, "Gilbert and the Color Orange," aloud to the whole group:
- Gilbert hated the color orange. He learned to hate it when he was a young child. In fact, he couldn't remember a time when he didn't hate it.

    Now Gilbert had never actually been around anything that was orange. He certainly didn't have anything orange in his house. But his parents and the rest of his family hated orange, so Gilbert knew the color was not to be trusted.

    Gilbert went through life avoiding orange. He never tasted the juicy sections of the orange fruit or smelled an orange flower. He never drew with an orange crayon or wore an orange shirt. He never carved an orange pumpkin or watched the sun set in an orange sky. For Gilbert, orange pop, orange sherbet, and orange candy were out.

    In high school, the rest of Gilbert's friends signed up for the basketball team, but Gilbert stayed home. The idea of dribbling an orange basketball down the court made him shudder. "Why don't the others understand how horrible orange is?" Gilbert thought.

    Because Gilbert hated orange, he missed out on a lot. He feared the color and kept away from it whenever he could. In fact, Gilbert grew to be an old man without ever really tasting or touching or smelling any of the enjoyable orange things in the world.

2. Make these comments about the story:
- Gilbert's attitude toward the color orange in the story above is called prejudice—that is, Gilbert pre-judged the color orange before he ever had a chance to know, from experience, what it was like.

    Sometimes we are prejudiced against individuals or groups of people. We pre-judge them without any evidence from personal experience to tell us what they are really like. Our prejudices are unreasoned and sometimes unreasonable. They can hurt us and others.

3. Lead a large-group discussion of the following questions:
- Have you every pre-judged a person wrongly? Explain.
- What made you jump to false conclusions about that person?
- What eventually made you change your mind about that person?
- Describe a time when you were a victim of prejudice.

    Invite the whole group to call out factors that contribute to prejudice as well as factors that help to eliminate it. Write these on newsprint.

4. Conclude the activity by conveying the following ideas in your own words:
- Prejudice hurts all of us. Gilbert missed out on a lot of life because of his prejudice against the color orange. We, too, miss out when we are victims of prejudice or when we are prejudiced against others. Jesus hung around with all types of people. He encourages us, by his example, to get to know many people, even those who appear different from us. Being a peacemaker means not being prejudiced.

(Adapted from Fletcher, *Teaching Peace*, pp. 29–30)

The Factory

Large-Group Activity (15 minutes)

This activity helps the retreatants recognize the difference between responding to *symptoms* of a problem and responding to the *cause* of a problem.

1. Divide the teens into three groups of roughly equal size. Give these instructions in your own words:
- In the following story, people begin to see that there is a problem and try to do something about it. As you listen, try to decide what you think should be done.

    Whenever I say the word *people,* I want everyone to stomp their feet. Group 1, whenever I say the word *machine* or *machinery,* please make the sound of a machine. Group 2, whenever I say the word *accident,* please whine in pain. Group 3, whenever I say the word *hospital,* please make a siren sound.

2. Read the following story aloud:
- There was once a factory where thousands of *people* worked. Its production line was a miracle of modern engineering. It turned out thousands of *machines* each day. But the factory had many *accidents*. The *machinery* just was not safe.

Day after day *people* came out of the factory with injuries resulting from many *accidents*. Some *people* came out with squashed fingers or cuts and bruises from the *machinery*. Other *people* lost an arm or a leg. Occasionally someone was crushed to death by the *machinery*.

Soon *people* began to see that something needed to be done. First on the scene were the churches. A priest set up a small first-aid tent outside the factory gate. With the help of the council of churches, the first-aid station grew into a proper clinic. The clinic was able to give first aid and to treat quite serious *accidents*.

The town council became interested, and local charity groups helped out. The clinic grew into a small *hospital* with modern equipment, an operating room, and full-time doctors and nurses. The lives of many *people* were saved.

Finally the factory owners saw the good that was being done. They wanted to show that they cared, so they gave the *hospital* their official support with unlimited access to the factory, a small amount of money, and an ambulance to speed victims of serious *accidents* from the factory to the *hospital*.

But each year the number of *accidents* got higher. More and more *people* were hurt. And in spite of everything the *hospital* did, more and more *people* died. Only then did some *people* begin to ask if it was enough to treat people's injuries while leaving untouched the *machinery* that caused them.

3. Lead a discussion with the whole group based on these questions:
- What was the problem in the factory?
- What did people do to deal with the problem?
- How do you feel about what they did? What would you have chosen to do?
- Did the way people acted help to change the cause of the problem (change) or help to deal with the results of the problem (charity)? What kind of approach would have been better in the long run? What might the priest have done first?
- What kind of things could have been done by the workers, the factory owners, and the community members to help change this situation?
- In what world situations do you think charity is important? change is important? both change and charity are important?
- Can you think of a situation in your own community or school in which charity is important? in which change is important? in which both charity and change are important?

4. Here are two further situations:
- Every summer Sanitown has a problem with a polluted beach. Donations are being collected to build a swimming pool.
- The school in Biggerton has a big problem with vandalism. The principal of the school announces tough new rules to suspend anyone caught destroying property.

Conclude by asking this question:
- Are the solutions proposed a response to immediate need? Are they likely to change the situation?

(Adapted from Huntly, *Rich World, Poor World,* pp. 175, 185)

Lunch   (45 minutes)

Icebreakers   (10–15 minutes)

Choose from among the icebreakers offered in part A of the appendix of this book, or use games of your own.

World Simulation Game   Large-Group Activity (45 minutes)

This activity makes the retreatants aware of effects of the unequal distribution of resources in our world.

1. Make a large square on the floor with masking tape (approximately 20 feet by 20 feet). Divide the square in half. One-half will represent the small percentage of the world's population living in the uppermost income bracket. Label this section Group A. Divide the remaining half into one-third and two-thirds. The two-thirds section will represent the people who are able to afford the basic necessities of providing for their family. Label this section Group B. The one-third section will represent the three-quarters of the world's population who live in poor countries. Label this section Group C.

Note: In the past, the terms First World, Second World, and Third World were used to describe countries. Today these terms are no longer adequate because a huge gap exists between the very rich and the very poor in almost every country. This game helps the teens understand the unequal distribution of resources, even in their own country.

Assign the teens to groups in the following way: Put 10 percent of the young people in Group A, 25 percent in Group B, and 65 percent in Group C. (You can do this by having the teens take slips of colored construction paper. Group A equals red; Group B equals blue; Group C equals yellow.)

2. Explain the object of the game this way:
- The goal of this exercise is to create a collage. The team with the best collage wins a prize.

After the teens have moved to their respective areas, ask them to guess what their group represents. Then say:
- We have divided you into groups based on economic status. Group A represents the small percentage of the population living in the uppermost income bracket. These people are extravagant in their consumption. They can afford the best health care and education, and their future is secure. Group B represents the people who are able to afford the basic necessities of providing for their family. They have fairly secure jobs, and their children look forward to growing up and getting a decent education and job. They are able to go to the doctor when they are sick. Group C represents the approximately three-quarters of the world's population who live in poor countries. These people generally lack access to good health care, education, and employment. These people live with little hope of a better future.

Point out that in the United States, as elsewhere, people from all three of these groups are represented.

3. After the groups have been identified, invite each group to see if it can figure out why a certain number of people have been chosen for each world. The answer is that each person represents a unit of population.

4. Then raise these questions to the group as a whole:
- How do you feel standing in your designated space?
- How does too many or too few people per land area affect a group?
- If having too many people causes poverty, which group is the richest? the poorest?

Be sure to make this point:
- Due to poverty and malnutrition, many children either die or are permanently damaged.

5. Designate the following handicaps: cloths tied over mouths for mute people, blindfolds over eyes for blind people, and string tied around hands for bound people. In Group A, designate one person as mute. In Group B, make one person mute and one blind. In Group C, make two people mute, two blind, and two with hands bound.

6. Next, pose the following questions for discussion:
- Can you explain why many parents in Group B and Group C countries often have many children? or why people in Group A countries typically have fewer children?
- What role do children play in each group?
- Can you list some positive changes that would affect the poverty and birth and death rates in these groups? [Some possible answers include good medical facilities, access to education, employment, old-age security, adequate food.]

7. Direct each group to choose one person to be the "government." This person is in charge and makes all final decisions. Distribute the wealth as follows (if possible distribute chairs and tables in addition to the art supplies): Group A—two small tables or one large table and enough chairs for each person, two pieces of poster board, ten magazines, two bottles of glue, a scissors, pipe cleaners, stickers, and the like; Group B—one table and half the number of chairs needed, one piece of poster board, five magazines, one bottle of glue, a scissors; Group C—two chairs, two magazines.

Then ask this question:
- What do the chairs and art supplies represent?

After establishing that they represent the relative wealth of each world, you might introduce the idea of the Gross National Product. Explain that the GNP is a figure representing the wealth of a country. It is a measure of the value of what is produced, consumed, imported, and exported by that country in a given period.

Next, ask these questions:
- Based on the distribution of art supplies, which group has the highest GNP? the lowest?
- Can you think of some reasons that this is so?

List the reasons on newsprint. You may suggest some of the following reasons:

• Many countries do not receive money for their exports.
• Some countries have a lot of industry.
• Some countries spend a lot on their military.
• Some countries do not have enough resources to meet the needs of their people.

Now allow time for each group to make a collage with the theme of peace, using the supplies they have been given.

8. About 10 minutes before the exercise is to end, give out candy to each government representative, something like licorice that can be broken apart. Distribute the candy as follows: Group A—one to two pieces per person; Group B—half the number of pieces as people in the group; Group C—one quarter the number of pieces as people in the group.

Instruct the government representatives to distribute the candy as follows:

• The government keeps half for its share; the next person gets half of the rest; the next person gets half of what is left, and so on until each person has a portion.

9. Afterward, raise these questions for discussion:

• How well did the poor do in your group (the last to receive) compared with the rich (the first to receive)?
• How did the poor people in your group do compared with the poor people in other groups?
• How did you feel when the candy was distributed?
• Was the candy distributed fairly?
• Why shouldn't every person have been given the same number of pieces of candy?
• What way would you have divided the candy?

10. Give the teens the final 10 minutes to complete their collages. Judge the collages when they are done and award the winners a prize.

Then ask these questions:

• What did you like about the game? What did you dislike?
• Was the game fair?
• What could we have done to make the game more fair?
• What does this game teach us?

11. Have a volunteer read Acts 2:42–47, about sharing everything. Then lead a discussion with the whole group based on the following questions:

• What does this exercise say about poverty and wealth?
• What makes it easy to share? What makes it difficult?
• Is it possible for the world to be more equal? Why or why not?
• What would it take for the world to become more equal?

(Adapted from Huntly, *Rich World, Poor World,* pp. 67–70)

Front Page   Small-Group Activity (15 minutes)

This activity helps the retreatants see that they have the ability to make the world a better place.

Direct the teens to form small groups. Give each small group a copy of resource 3–A, "Front Page," to complete.

Instruct the group using words similar to the following:

• Every day we see the negative things that happen in our world. In your small group, pretend that you are a group of journalists writing the front page of a newspaper ten years from now. On this front page you are to create pictures and stories about people making positive changes in our world. For example, one headline could be "Cure for AIDS Discovered."

The story might read: "Today the *New England Journal of Medicine* reported that a cure for AIDS has been discovered. When asked to comment, Dr. Nopain said, 'Ten years ago we hoped that we would discover this cure, and we are truly thankful that this cure will now be available. This tremendous feat could not have been achieved without the exceptional generosity and perseverance of numerous people: those who gave donations, those who volunteered their time, those who prayed, and those who by their tireless dedication completed the research.'"

Allow enough time for the small groups to complete their front page. When they are finished, invite each small group to read and display its front page.

Conclude the activity by asking if anyone has any additional comments to make.

Spiral of Peace

Affirmation (15–20 minutes)

In this activity the retreatants affirm themselves for the qualities they possess that enable them to be peacemakers.

Form small groups. Give each person a copy of resource 3–B, "Spiral of Peace." Explain these directions to the small groups:

• Write your name in the center of the spiral. Then, in the other rings of the spiral, write the names of the people whom you care about and love. Also write or draw pictures of the gifts and talents God has given you. Then write down ways you are a peacemaker already or how you would like to be a peacemaker.

After everyone has finished writing and drawing, direct them to cut out their spiral by cutting along the solid lines. Tell the teens to punch a hole in their spiral and to run a piece of string through the hole in order to hang it.

Invite each person to share with her or his small group what she or he wrote or drew.

Closing Guided Meditation

(20–30 minutes)

Begin the meditation with a progressive muscle relaxation exercise (see part C of the appendix for suggestions). If possible, play soft instrumental background music. Then continue with the following guided meditation. Pause for a few seconds at each ellipsis (. . .).

• It is said, "Peace begins within each one of us." When we are at peace, those around us can be at peace also. Jesus is called the Prince of Peace because he remained focused on God and God's love. That love guided him in his decisions and invited people to make the world a peace-filled place.

Imagine yourself high above the earth on a cloud. . . . The cloud is very soft. . . . Any aches or pains you felt seem to go away because of the softness. . . . The cloud is as soft as a puppy's fur and as warm as a favorite blanket. . . . Here on this cloud you feel very safe and secure. . . .

Now the cloud takes you to a place where people are not at peace. . . . See the people. . . . What are they doing that shows you they are not at peace? [Longer pause.] Feel the tension. . . . Now see Jesus come into the picture. . . . What is Jesus doing to bring peace? [Longer pause.] See the people calm down. . . . Jesus invites you to say something to these people. . . . What is it you want to tell them? [Longer pause.]

Jesus now takes you to a peace-filled place. . . . Where does he take you? What makes it peace filled? [Longer pause.] Jesus says: "Peace isn't always easy. . . . We often hurt one another's feelings because we say things we don't really mean. . . . I came to earth to tell you about forgiveness. When we are hurt, or when we hurt others, we need to talk to them and correct the situation and seek forgiveness." . . .

Jesus asks you, "Is there anything you've done recently that was not peaceful and that hurt yourself or others? Spend some time talking with Jesus, knowing that he loves you very much and wants to listen to you. [Longer pause.]

Jesus says, "I forgive you. . . . Now you must go and ask for forgiveness. . . . I will give you the strength you need to do it." [Longer pause.]

Now Jesus asks you, "What have you done recently that has brought peace to another person or situation?" [Longer pause.]

Jesus continues: "You, too, are an instrument of peace because you are one of my followers. . . . It isn't easy to be a person of peace in our violent and troubled world. . . . Anytime you feel angry or upset, calm yourself down and I will be with you to talk and pray." . . .

Before Jesus leaves, is there anything else you want to say to him? [Longer pause.] Jesus concludes his time with you by saying: "Thank you for being with me today and for sharing with me. . . . I will continue to pray for you and guide you in being an instrument of peace."

Jesus turns and walks away. . . . You take this time to say a prayer: "God, thank you for sending us Jesus. He faced many hurtful situations but was able to bring peace to many people. Help me to be a peacemaker. Guide me in all that I do. Help me believe that peace is possible and that peace begins with me. Amen."

When you open your eyes, you will no longer be on the cloud but back here in this room. When you are ready, slowly open your eyes and come back.

Evaluation

Large Group (5 minutes)

After the guided meditation, direct the teens to reflect in writing on the following questions. Invite them to answer aloud if they feel comfortable doing so.

- If you had only one word to describe today, what word would you pick?
- What is one new thing you learned today, or what is one thing you really liked? (It could be something we did or something someone said.)
- What do you feel God is challenging you to do as a result of this retreat?

But I Say to You

Popular Wisdom Suggests	Wisdom of Jesus Responds
1. Take good care of yourself. Watch out for number one.	2 Corinthians 8:8–15
2. Charity begins at home.	James 2:14–17
3. The little I can do will not make a difference.	Mark 12:41–44
4. The one who gets the most toys wins!	Matthew 19:16–30
5. Invest for tomorrow.	Luke 12:13–21
6. Keep to your own group; avoid those in need.	Matthew 25:31–46

(Thomas Bright, editor, *Poverty: Do It Justice!* [New Rochelle, NY: Don Bosco Multimedia, 1993], page 90)

Handout 3–A: Permission to reproduce this handout for use in your program is granted.

Front Page

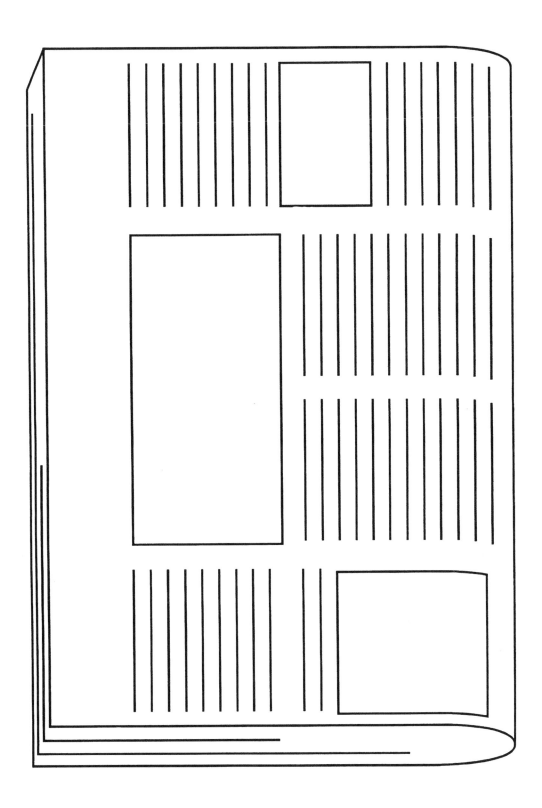

Resource 3–A: Permission to reproduce this resource for use in your program is granted.

63

Spiral of Peace

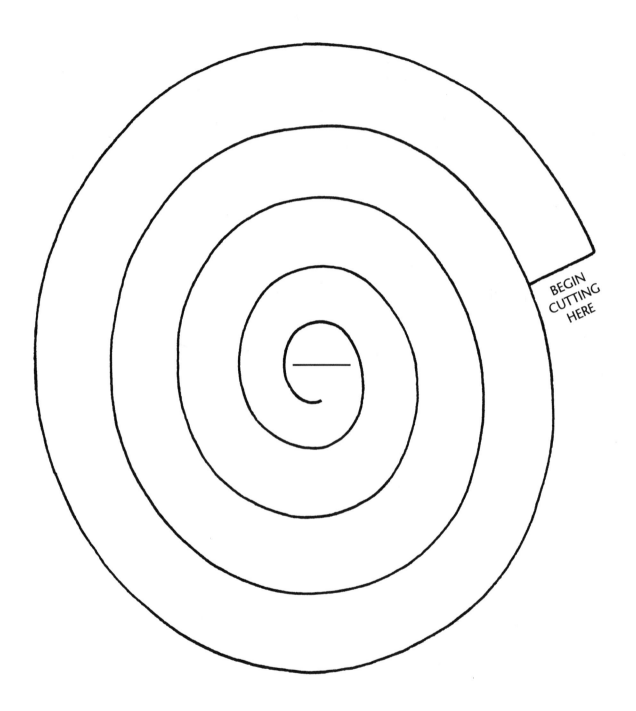

BEGIN
CUTTING
HERE

Resource 3–B: Permission to reproduce this resource for use in your program is granted.

Retreat 4

Peer Pressure

Theme   This retreat focuses on what peer pressure is, why we give in to negative peer pressure, and what we can do to resist it.

Bible Basis   *Luke 15:11–18.* In the parable of the prodigal son, we learn how peer pressure can lead people to make poor choices as well as good choices and that with God's help we can learn from our mistakes and make decisions for ourselves.

Objectives   The retreatants will do the following:
- identify various peer pressures, both positive and negative
- explore what motivates people to resist or succumb to negative peer pressure
- examine how people in the Scriptures resisted negative peer pressure
- practice strategies for resisting peer pressure through role-plays

Retreat at a Glance

The following chart offers a brief overview of the retreat activities, time frames, and materials needed. For more detailed information about any of the activities, refer to the directions given in the Retreat in Detail section.

ACTIVITY	TIME FRAME	SUPPLIES
Welcome and Introduction	10–15 minutes	poster with standards
Icebreakers	15–30 minutes	depends on selection
Opening Prayer	5 minutes	Bible
Balloon Pressures	15 minutes	balloons, permanent markers, index cards, pen or pencil
Peer Pressure Survey	15–20 minutes	paper, markers, masking tape
Motives and Consequences	45 minutes	Bibles, newsprint, markers
Break	10 minutes	
Different Tastes	15 minutes	4 different kinds of candy, plates, station signs
Christian Communications Commission	25–30 minutes	poster board, magazines, markers, tape, glue
Lunch	45 minutes	
Icebreakers	15 minutes	depends on selection
Holy Pressure	20 minutes	Bibles, paper, pencils, newsprint, markers
Timed Temptations	10–15 minutes	newsprint, markers, Bible, prizes
Ben's Party	30–45 minutes	resource 4–A, temptations list, newsprint, markers
Name Affirmation	15–20 minutes	markers, crayons, newsprint or butcher paper, masking tape
Closing Guided Meditation	20–30 minutes	instrumental music, tape or CD player
Evaluation	5 minutes	pencils, paper

Retreat in Detail

Welcome and Introduction

(10–15 minutes)

Icebreakers

(15–30 minutes)
Choose from among the icebreakers offered in part A of the appendix of this book, or use games of your own.

Opening Prayer

(5 minutes)
Begin by reading Luke 15:11–18—the parable of the prodigal son. Finish with a prayer similar to this one:
- Dear God, today we are confronted by many pressures—the glamour of wealth that encourages people to steal or lie; the excitement of foolish behaviors related to sex, drugs, and dangerous risk taking; and the pressure to ignore trusted adults while believing the false promises of the media.

  God, guide us in making wise decisions. Give us the strength to resist negative peer pressures and the courage to promote positive peer pressure. Amen.

Balloon Pressures

Small-Group Activity (15 minutes)
The purpose of this activity is to identify positive and negative areas of pressure and to visually demonstrate how pressure builds up.

Form the participants into small groups. Introduce the activity this way:
- Balloon Pressures is played like the popular game "Pictionary" except you will be drawing on balloons instead of paper. Each group will receive one large inflated balloon and a marker (have extra balloons on hand in case they are needed). Taking turns, each person in each group is to draw on the balloon a picture depicting a secret word. The other group members are to guess the secret word or phrase. All groups will receive the same secret word at the same time. The first group to call out the correct answer receives one point. Here are the rules:
  ○ The artist may not talk or make sounds.
  ○ The artist may not use hand gestures.
  ○ The artist may not use numbers or letters in his or her drawing.

  Give a permanent marker to the person with the longest last name in each small group. These will be the first set of artists. The artists come up to the front of the room, and simultaneously you give them each the secret word or phrase (have the secret words written on 3-by-5-inch cards, with enough sets of each word for all small groups). The artists then run back to their group and begin drawing on their balloon. Continue until everyone has had at least one chance to draw.

  Here are some secret words you could use: smoking, movies, lying, church, alcohol, sports, school, teachers, parents, straight A's, cheerleading, cafeteria, school bus.

  Lead a discussion with the whole group based on the following questions (see page 12 of the introduction for alternative ways of debriefing this and other retreat activities):

- Which of the words you drew described something that is often the result of negative peer pressure? [Smoking, lying, and the like]
- Which words described something that was the result of positive peer pressure? [Participating in church, sports, and the like]
  In your own words offer this conclusion to the activity:
- Sometimes peer pressure makes us feel trapped—like the air in a balloon. Our friends pressure us to be just like them, and we have a hard time saying no. In order to overcome negative peer pressure, we need to find ways to say no without losing our friends. That's what we hope to do today.

Peer Pressure Survey

Large-Group Activity (15–20 minutes)
In this activity the retreatants discover how other teens their age feel about the various pressures in their life.

Put 8½-by-11-inch pieces of paper on the floor or wall, each marking off a separate location. Write 10 percent on the first sheet and add increments of 10 percent to each succeeding piece, up to 80 percent.

Introduce the activity this way:
- The Boys and Girls Clubs of America took a nationwide survey of nearly 3,300 club members age thirteen to eighteen. I would like you to try and guess what the results were. After I read each statement, please stand by the percentage that you feel is the correct answer.
  ○ How many teens felt pressure to not do well in school? [40 percent]
  ○ How many felt pressure to cut classes? [50 percent, but 80 percent said they seldom did]
  ○ How many felt pressure to have sex? [40 percent]
  ○ How many felt pressure to drink alcohol? [40 percent]
  ○ How many felt pressure to commit minor crimes? [30 percent]
  ○ How many felt pressure to take drugs? [30 percent]
  ○ How many felt pressure to join a gang? [20 percent]
  Here's another side to the picture:
  ○ How many were confident of their ability to get a good education? [70 percent]
  ○ How many were confident of their ability to have a good family life? [70 percent]
  ○ How many were confident of their ability to get a good job? [70 percent]
      (Statistics cited in *Youthworker Update,* November 1990, p. 4. These statistics were rounded off to the nearest ten percent.)
  Lead a large-group discussion of the following questions:
- Did any of the statistics surprise you? If so, why?
- Which statistic was the most significant to you and why?

Motives and Consequences

Small-Group Activity (45 minutes)
This activity highlights the various motivations people have for making decisions. The activity is based loosely on Lawrence Kohlberg's stages of moral development.

1. Begin by dividing the young people into three small groups. Give each small group a Bible and ask them to open it to Luke 15:11–20.

Assign the first group verses 11 through 12, assign the second group verse 13, and assign the third group verses 14 through 20. Give these directions in your own words:

• Each small group has been assigned a passage from the Scriptures. It is your job to create a role-play around that section of the passage— and only that section. Be as creative as possible. Each person must play a part in the role-play.

Allow the groups enough time to prepare. After each group has performed its role-play, ask the presenting group these two questions:

• What motivated the main character to do what he did?
• What were or could be the consequences of his actions?

2. When all the small groups have presented their role-play and answered the questions, teach them the following information about levels of motivation:

• People are motivated to do things for a variety of reasons. At the lowest level, which we will call level three, people do things because they feel like it. People act spontaneously and impulsively. Because they make their decision quickly, little thought is given to the result of their actions.

At the next level, which we will call level two, people do things because they are pressured to do them by someone or something else. For example, people might feel the pressure to be popular or to achieve financial success. Their decisions are based on influences outside themselves.

At the highest level, which we will call level one, people do things because they have taken the time to think about the decision and its possible effects on other people. The decision is based on their values.

3. Designate one section of the room as level one, another as level two, and another as level three. In your own words, give the group the following directions:

• After I read each scenario, move to the section of the room that designates the level out of which you feel the main character acted. After you have moved, I will ask you to explain your decision.

Read aloud the following scenarios. Pause after each one to allow the retreatants to move to the appropriate spot. Then invite volunteers to explain the reasons for their choice.

  • Sam got so excited when he was declared valedictorian that he ran out of the cafeteria, screaming and jumping up and down.
  • Esmerelda wears the latest designer perfume because it is her boyfriend's favorite.
  • Melissa chooses to skip a big graduation party because she knows some of the kids will be doing drugs.
  • Bob chooses his Uncle Manny to be his confirmation sponsor because his uncle is rich, handsome, and popular.
  • Peter decides to spend his Easter break in Mexico building houses for the poor instead of joining his friends who are going to Disney World.

- Julia buys a chartreuse jacket because it looks good on the mannequin in the store window.

4. Move the participants back into their small groups. Distribute a sheet of newsprint and a marker to each group, and say something like this:
- Think of other situations in which people might act on these three levels. Brainstorm as a small group and write one scenario for each level. Have the group recorder be the person with the smallest shoe size.

Give the groups enough time to write their three scenarios. Then invite the recorders to read aloud their group's responses.

5. Offer a conclusion like the following to wrap up the activity:
- Knowing there are different levels upon which to make decisions can help us make better choices, especially when we are confronted with negative peer pressure. Thinking about the consequences of our choices can enable us to make wise decisions.

Break (10 minutes)

Different Tastes

Large-Group Activity (15 minutes)

This activity shows the retreatants that it is possible to have strong friendships with others even if some of their interests are different.

Bring enough candy for all the young people. Include four different kinds. Place each kind of candy on a separate plate in a different location. Number the locations from 1 to 4, and make a sign identifying the number of each station. For example:
- *Station 1.* Life Savers candy
- *Station 2.* Milky Way bars
- *Station 3.* Kit Kat bars
- *Station 4.* gummy bears

1. Instruct the retreatants to walk around the room and look at the different kinds of candy. Then have them stand next to the kind they like best.

Introduce the activity in your own words:
- We often judge others based on what they wear, do, listen to, or eat. And sometimes we base friendships on the same things. You are now standing with people who like the same kind of candy as you do. This is your candy group. Don't eat the candy yet. I'm going to list some activities and interests you may have. For each, I'll direct you to stand near one of the numbered stations. After I read the options, please move to the appropriate station.

Pause after each question. The retreatants will probably move several times.
- Which sport do you like best? If track, move to station 1. If football, move to station 2. If basketball, move to station 3. If you don't like sports much, move to station 4.
- Which school subject do you like best? If math, move to station 1. If English, move to station 2. If science, move to station 3. If art, move to station 4.

- Which kind of movies do you like best? If mysteries, move to station 1. If comedies, move to station 2. If dramas, move to station 3. If adventures or thrillers, move to station 4.
- Which musical style do you like best? If heavy metal, move to station 1. If popular rock, move to station 2. If rap or alternative, move to station 3. If country or reggae, move to station 4.

After the last question, tell the teens they may have one piece of candy from the station at which they ended up. Then have them sit down.

2. Discuss the following question:
- With how many people outside your original candy group did you have other things in common?

3. Conclude the activity by expressing these thoughts in your own words:
- Imagine how many friendships you might miss out on if you base your friendships solely on one thing—such as what kind of candy you like or your favorite music.

Many times we give in to peer pressure to please our friends, because we want to be like them. By doing this we can shortchange ourselves and our friends. By being exposed to different hobbies, foods, values, and ideas—and also to a variety of friends—we can grow in ways we never thought possible.

(Adapted from Parolini, ed., *Today's Music: Good or Bad?* pp. 27–28)

Christian Communications Commission

Small-Group Activity (25–30 minutes)

This activity helps the retreatants understand the strong pressures the media impose on us.

1. Divide the large group into four small groups. Give each small group a sheet of poster board, several magazines, markers, tape, and glue. Assign one of the following pressures to each small group: being sexually active, using alcohol or cigarettes, having a perfect body, and having a lot of money.

Introduce the activity this way:
- Your small group is the CCC, Christian Communications Commission. Each small group is to work on the pressure it has been assigned. Search the magazines for ads with messages that promote your particular pressure. Find as many as you can and glue them onto your poster board.

2. Allow enough time for the groups to complete the assignment. When the groups appear finished, invite them to share their posters. Then ask the whole group:
- Why are the ads' messages so inviting?
- As Christians, how can we respond to these pressures?

3. Continue the activity by instructing the group:
- Now your small group must create an ad depicting resistance to these pressures. You can use magazine pictures or create your own drawings.

When the groups are finished, have them share their ads.

4. Conclude the activity with these words:
• Everywhere we look there are messages that influence us. The job of advertisers is to make money, even though advertisers claim that their job is to make you feel better or more popular. We don't have to give in to these powerful messages.

Lunch (45 minutes)

Icebreakers (15 minutes)
Choose from among the icebreakers offered in part A of the appendix of this book, or use games of your own.

Holy Pressure Small-Group Activity (20 minutes)
In this activity the retreatants look to the Scriptures for examples of people of faith who encountered peer pressure.

Form the participants into small groups of up to eight people. Give this introduction to the activity:
• Peer pressure has been around as long as people have been on the earth. The Scriptures contain several examples of people being subjected to the pressures of the day. In this activity each small group reads about and reflects on one particular person from the Scriptures.

Assign a different one of the following Scripture passages to each small group:
• *Gen. 6:9–22.* Noah builds the ark.
• *Exod. 32:1–8.* The Israelites worship a golden idol.
• *Matt. 1:18–25.* Joseph planned to break his engagement to Mary.
• *Luke 1:46–56.* Mary praises the Lord.
• *Luke 4:1–13.* Jesus is tempted by the devil.
• *Luke 13:10–17.* Jesus heals on the Sabbath.
• *Luke 17:11–19.* One cured leper returns to thank Jesus.
• *Luke 18:1–5.* The widow appears before the judge.

Direct the small groups to read their Scripture passage and discuss the reflection questions as a group. Post the following reflection questions on newsprint where they can be seen by everyone:
• How was this person faithful to himself or herself and to God?
• What do you think society thought of this person or said about her or him?
• How did this person deal with peer pressure?

Each small group needs a reporter. Select someone who hasn't been a leader yet. Give the groups time to read their passage and answer the questions.

Invite the reporter from each small group to give a brief summary of what his or her group discussed. Record the answers to the third question on newsprint.

Conclude the activity by conveying these ideas in your own words:
• On the newsprint are some qualities and strategies that can prepare us to deal with pressures that cannot be avoided. What are some of the pressures we face that cannot be avoided?

Timed Temptations Small-Group Activity (10–15 minutes)

This activity identifies temptations that teens often face.

Maintain the same small groups as in the previous activity. Give each small group a sheet of newsprint and a marker. Assign a recorder and a reporter in each group. The recorder is the person whose birthday is closest to Christmas, and the reporter is the person whose birthday is closest to the Fourth of July.

Give the following instructions in your own words:

• Your task is to list on newsprint the temptations that teens your age encounter. List as many temptations as possible. You will have 3 minutes to do this. The small group with the most temptations listed after 3 minutes will receive a prize. All answers must be legibly written by the recorder. If an answer isn't really a temptation, it won't be counted. If you list the same or similar idea more than once, it will be counted only once.

Start the activity by shouting "Go"! After 3 minutes, call time. Invite the reporters to bring their newsprint to the front of the room and take turns reading off their list of temptations. For questionable items, ask the entire group to vote on whether to accept the item. Then count the number of items on each team's list, declare the winner, and distribute prizes.

Call for a volunteer to read aloud 1 Cor. 10:13. After the reading say something like the following to conclude the activity:

• The Scriptures remind us that God will give us the strength we need to handle temptation. In the next activity we will learn some strategies for resisting temptation and negative peer pressure.

Ben's Party Small-Group Activity (30–45 minutes)

This activity encourages the teens to explore what causes people to give in to negative peer pressure, and it helps the teens develop strategies for resisting such pressure.

1. Invite seven volunteers to be part of a skit. Give them each a copy of resource 4–A, "Ben's Party." Practice the skit with them briefly. Then direct them to perform the skit in front of the whole group. Applaud at the end of the skit.

2. Discuss these questions with the whole group:
• What made some of the characters in the skit give in to the pressure? How did others resist?
• What can we learn about peer pressure from each of the characters?

3. Invite the teens to return to the same small groups they were in for the Timed Temptations activity. Give them this task:
• Design a role-play around one of the temptations your group came up with in the Timed Temptations activity. The main character should resist giving in to the pressure exerted by others. Everyone in your group must participate in the role-play.

Give the groups time to practice. Then ask them to perform their role-plays one at a time. Applaud at the end of each role-play.

4. After all the role-plays have been performed, discuss these questions with the whole group:
- What strategies did the main character use to resist negative peer pressure? [List these on newsprint.]
- Which strategies worked well? Which ones didn't work well? Why?
- What could the main character have done differently in order to be more successful at resisting the temptation?
- How likely are you to use these resistance strategies? Why or why not?
- Are there any other strategies that you or others have used that are not listed here? If so, what are they?

Name Affirmation

(15–20 minutes)

This activity reinforces positive qualities about each teen, using his or her name as a starting point.

Set out a variety of colored markers and crayons. Give each teen a piece of large paper, for example, butcher paper, construction paper, or newsprint. Direct the retreatants to creatively write their first and last name in large letters vertically down the left side of the paper. Tape the papers to the wall.

Give the following directions:
- Move around the room filling in affirming adjectives that start with a letter in a person's name and that describe the person named on the paper. Only one adjective is allowed per each letter of the name.

It is important that all the teens have something written on their piece of paper. This may require you to write some adjectives on the less popular teens' papers or to quietly encourage other teens to make sure all the retreatants have a complete affirmation.

(Adapted from Rice, *Up Close and Personal,* p. 71)

Closing Guided Meditation

(20–30 minutes)

Begin the meditation with a progressive muscle relaxation exercise (see part C of the appendix for suggestions). If possible, play soft instrumental background music. Then continue with the following guided meditation. Pause for a few seconds at each ellipsis (. . .).

- All peer pressure isn't bad. Many times our friends encourage us to pursue a goal, develop a talent, or try a new hobby. Yet we also know that we are pressured to engage in unhealthy things. Jesus invites us to get our strength from him to resist negative peer pressure.

    Imagine yourself at a big state fair. . . . There are all kinds of rides to go on, many booths of games to play, and various vendors selling things to eat. . . . A lot of excitement is in the air. . . . Everyone appears to be enjoying themselves. . . . You see some of your friends and join them for something to eat. . . . Together you go on a favorite ride. . . . Afterward someone suggests leaving the fair and going to buy alcohol and drugs. . . . Another friend says, "No one will know, and we will be back to the fair before it closes." You don't like what's happening. . . . You feel uncomfortable. . . . You don't want to insult or confront your friends, but you also don't want to go with them. . . .

Just then a special friend joins you—it's Jesus. . . . He is young and dresses a lot like you and your friends. . . . As soon as he joins your group, you feel more relaxed and confident. . . . You tell your friends you are going to stay at the fair with your friend Jesus. . . .

Jesus invites you to walk with him away from the noisy area of the fair to a quieter section. . . .

Jesus says: "Tell me about a time when you resisted negative peer pressure. . . . How did you feel before and after?" Take some time to share with Jesus. [Longer pause.] "If you had to do it again, what would you do the same? . . . What would you do differently?" [Longer pause.]

Jesus continues: "It isn't always easy to resist, but we can learn a lot from times when we do resist and times when we give in. . . . Can you tell me about a time when you gave in to peer pressure. How did it feel?" [Longer pause.]

Jesus adds: "We all make mistakes. . . . It is those who learn from their mistakes that we call heroes. . . . Tell me about a time you 'pressured,' or a better word might be *supported,* someone into doing the right thing. . . . How did it feel?" [Longer pause.]

Jesus continues: "Tell me about a time when someone pressured you into doing the right thing. . . . How did you feel?" [Longer pause.]

Jesus reminds you that life is filled with pressures, and that he is always with you to guide you if you let him. . . . God has given you many gifts and traits. . . . Jesus asks, "What is one quality that you're proud of that helps you resist negative peer pressure?" [Longer pause.]

Before Jesus goes, he asks you if there is anything else you would like to talk to him about? . . . Spend these last few moments talking and listening to Jesus. [Longer pause.]

Jesus explains that it is time for him to go, and he hopes you and he can get together again soon. . . . Jesus leaves, and as he does, you look up into the sky and see a very bright star. You decide to say a little prayer: "Jesus, thank you for always being with me, guiding me, and forgiving me. Help me to be a person who supports others in doing good rather than bad, and give me the strength to resist temptations that are not healthy or wise. Amen."

When you open your eyes, you will no longer be at the fair but back here in this room. When you are ready, slowly open your eyes and come back.

Evaluation

Large Group (5 minutes)

After the guided meditation, invite the teens to reflect in writing on the following questions. Tell them that they may answer aloud if they feel comfortable doing so.

- If you had only one word to describe today, what word would you pick?
- What is one new thing you learned today, or what is one thing you really liked? (It could be something we did or something someone said.)
- What do you feel God is challenging you to do as a result of this retreat?

Ben's Party

Characters: Narrator, Walter Wimp, Macho Mike, Sylvia Snob, Curious Carol, Christine Confident, and Ben, an older student

Narrator. This is a story about negative peer pressure. After school one day, Ben sees five younger students. One at a time, he invites them to his party.

Ben. Hi Sylvia, want to be a part of the "in crowd" and come to my big party Saturday night?

Sylvia. *[Whispers to herself: Well, I don't want to go because I don't know what will happen, but I can't let him know I'm afraid.]* You are so stupid to think I'd fall for a joke like that. Besides I wouldn't be caught dead with someone as ugly as you. I'm not coming.

Ben. Hey, Walter, my man, I know you want to come to my party. Lots of girls, a little booze, and you'll be feeling GREAAAAT!

Walter. I don't think I should come. We might get caught.

Ben. O come on, you little wimp, everyone else is coming. You know you really want to come.

Walter. Oh, all right.

Ben. Hey, Mike, you like to hang with all of us older guys, why don't you come to my party?

Mike. Well if everyone else is going to be there, I'll be there too. I'm sure everyone will want to see me. *[Ben and Mike do a high-five.]*

Ben. Hi, Carol, listen, how would you . . .

Carol. *[Interrupting Ben]* Your party sounds awesome, and I'm dying to come. I've never been to one before and I am just so curious. Nothing could stop me.

Ben. Well, some others seem hesitant, you know, they want to check it out with mommy and daddy.

Carol. Oh, I didn't even think of that, but I'm sure my parents will let me go when I tell them how curious I am and that I will just die from curiosity if I don't go.

Ben. Hey, Christine, you're the last one on my list of prestigious guests to come to my party.

Christine. *[Whispers to herself: I remember hearing about these parties and people getting drunk, getting hurt, and then being rushed to the hospital. Plus, if I get caught, I'll be grounded.]* No, someone could get hurt or we could get in trouble.

Ben. *[Laughing]* Chicken!

Christine. Think what you would like, but I have plans to go to my girlfriend Suzy's house where I know I'll have a nice, safe time. Nothing's going to spoil that!

Retreat 5

Self-Esteem

Theme   This retreat helps the retreatants to see themselves as unique individuals and to feel good about who God has made them to be.

Bible Basis   *Luke 19:1–10.* Like Zacchaeus, we, too, can learn that our self-esteem is not limited to our physical characteristics but is built on the gifts with which God has blessed us. God invites us to use those gifts to build up our own self-esteem and the self-esteem of others.

Objectives   The retreatants will do the following:
- examine the influence of advertising on their self-image
- define the word *self-esteem*
- explore the consequences of a negative self-image
- develop ways to boost their self-esteem
- reaffirm the belief that God loves each person unconditionally

Retreat at a Glance

The following chart offers a brief overview of the retreat activities, time frames, and materials needed. For more detailed information about any of the activities, refer to the directions given in the Retreat in Detail section.

ACTIVITY	TIME FRAME	SUPPLIES
Welcome and Introduction	10–15 minutes	poster with standards
Icebreakers	15–30 minutes	depends on selection
Opening Prayer	5 minutes	
Agree or Disagree?	10–15 minutes	
Media Me	15–20 minutes	newsprint, markers, Bible
Label Charades	15–20 minutes	labels, marker, tape
"I'm An Original" Bingo	20 minutes	handout 5–A, pencils
Complimentary Cupcakes	15 minutes plus 10-minute break	prepared cupcakes, pen, toothpick flags
Talents Sculpture	20–25 minutes	scrap paper, markers, masking tape
Self-Esteem Scramble	10–15 minutes	brown lunch bags, slips of paper, pen
Lunch	45 minutes	
Icebreakers	15 minutes	depends on selection
Zack and Me	20–30 minutes	paper clouds and stars, tape, Bible, handout 5–B, pencils
Skits	20–30 minutes	resource 5–A
Rebuilding Self-Esteem	20–30 minutes	sets of 8½-by-11-inch paper, markers, masking tape
Thumbs Up!	15–25 minutes	ink pads, handout 5–B, pencils, paper towels
Closing Guided Meditation	20–30 minutes	instrumental music, tape or CD player
Evaluation	5 minutes	pencils, paper

Retreat in Detail

Welcome and Introduction

(10–15 minutes)

Icebreakers

(15–30 minutes)
Choose from among the icebreakers offered in the appendix of this book, or use games of your own.

Opening Prayer

(5 minutes)
Begin the prayer by reading the following adaptation of a popular Scripture story:

- Jesus was going through the city of Jericho. A wealthy and important tax collector named Zacchaeus was there. He wanted to see Jesus but was unable to because he was too short to see above the crowd. Zacchaeus ran ahead to a place where Jesus would come, and he climbed a sycamore tree so he could see Jesus. When Jesus came to that place, Jesus looked up and said to him, "Zacchaeus, hurry and come down! I must stay at your house today." (Adapted from Luke 19:1–5)

  Finish with a prayer similar to this one:

- Dear God, just as Zacchaeus overcame obstacles to get to see you, help us overcome any obstacles that keep us from seeing you in our life. Bless us with the gift of enthusiasm to seek you that Zacchaeus had. Help us to understand that you are present here in others and in a special way in ourselves. Please help us to remember that we are special and unique because we are made in your image and likeness.

  Thank you for our life and for all the people who love us and build up our self-esteem. Amen.

Agree or Disagree?

Large-Group Activity (10–15 minutes)
This activity opens a discussion on the concept of self-esteem.

Designate one side of the room as "Agree," and the other side as "Disagree."

Give the group these instructions:

- I am going to read a series of statements, one at a time. If you agree with the statement, then stand in the "Agree" section. If you disagree, then stand in the "Disagree" section.

  After reading a statement, direct the teens to make their choice. Then call for volunteers to explain their choice. Add your own opinions if you feel they are necessary.

- The last thing I usually do before leaving home is look in the mirror.
- Good-looking people have more friends.
- People judge others by their physical attractiveness.
- It's okay to wear the latest fashions and fads.
- Sometimes I wish I looked like someone else.
- I don't let a person's appearance affect the way I think of him or her.
- God made me the way I am for a reason, so I should be happy with myself.
- In order to succeed in life, a person needs a positive self-image.

- People get their self-esteem from their family.
- My friends influence my self-esteem.
   Conclude the activity this way:
- Today we will be looking at what self-esteem is, where it comes from, and how we can restore it when it has been damaged.

Media Me

Small-Group Activity (15–20 minutes)

This activity highlights the effects that the media and advertising have on our self-image.

1. Form the retreatants into small groups. Give each small group a large piece of newsprint and some colored markers. Offer the teens directions similar to these:

- Each small group is to work together to create what the media tell us is the ideal person. To do this, draw a stick figure and dress up the figure using brand-name clothing and accessories. You may also include such items as deodorant and cologne. See how many items your group can put on your "ideal person." The team with the most number of items wins. Each group will need a recorder to record the items the team uses, an artist to dress up the figure, and a reporter to display the finished product and read off the items. The person in each group whose birthday is closest to today's date is the recorder, the shortest person is the artist, and the person whose birthday is closest to Christmas is the reporter.

   Give the small groups enough time to complete their picture. When everyone is finished, invite the reporters to share their group's picture aloud, stating the items and their brand names.

2. Process the activity with the whole group by using the following discussion questions (see page 12 of the introduction for alternative ways of debriefing this and other retreat activities):

- What made this activity easy or difficult? Why?
- What effects do the media and advertising have on our self-image?
- What makes it easy or difficult to believe what they say?
- Do you think most teenagers think they are beautiful or ugly? Explain.
- Why does our society sometimes discard imperfect things and keep perfect ones?

3. Next, read aloud Matt. 6:25–29. Then discuss the following questions:

- What does this passage say about self-esteem?
- What makes a person feel ideal or inferior?
- How do you deal with feeling inferior?
- How does God show us we are loved just the way we are?

4. Conclude the activity by expressing these ideas in your own words:

- It's often easier to see our imperfections than our strengths. But even though we feel ugly at times, God still loves us. God wants us to take care of our body, but we are not judged by God based on our physical appearance.

Label Charades

Small-Group Activity (15–20 minutes)
This activity identifies what it is that makes people famous.

Have labels prepared for this game. On each label write the name of one famous person, living or dead. For example, Moses, Virgin Mary, Noah, George Washington, Ben Franklin, Florence Nightingale, Amelia Earhart, Rosa Parks, Martin Luther King Jr., Tom Hanks, God, Cher, Julia Roberts, Whitney Houston, President Clinton, Hillary Rodham Clinton, Michael Jordan, and others.

1. Begin by asking the whole group this question:
- Who can tell me how you play charades?

    After receiving various responses from the teens, explain the way the game will be played:
- In a moment I will put a label on the back of each person. It will be the name of someone famous, living or dead. The other members in your small group must act out clues for you until you guess the famous person whose name you have on your back. The people doing the acting are not allowed to talk or make sounds. The first group finished wins.

2. Form small groups of equal size. Tape a label on each person's back. Give the signal for the groups to begin. Continue until everyone guesses who they are. If some small groups finish before others, offer them new labels to continue playing the game until everyone is done. Declare the winner.

3. Lead a large-group discussion based on the following questions:
- What makes people famous?
- Is there any connection between fame and self-esteem? If so, what is the connection?
- How did you feel when you didn't know your "identity"?
- Was it hard for you to discover the name on your back? Why or why not?
- How is this activity similar to our working on our self-esteem?

4. Offer this conclusion to the activity:
- You each had to interact with others to discover your label. In the same way, we each need others to help us discover who we are and to identify the things about us that make us special or unique.

"I'm An Original" Bingo

Large-Group Activity (20 minutes)
The purpose of this activity is to help the retreatants recognize that simple things can make us unique.

Give each person a copy of handout 5–A, "I'm an Original," and a pencil. Then explain the following directions:
- When I tell you to begin, find people in the room who fit the characteristics named on the handout and get them each to sign a different box. The first person to get Bingo (all blocks in a row signed—either horizontally, vertically, or diagonally) wins. You must find people who truly fit the description in a box. If a box describes an *action,* have the person perform the action before signing the box. *No one can sign the same paper more than once.* When you get Bingo, call

it out and bring your handout to me to check and determine who our winners are.

Begin the game. Continue until you have several winners.

At the end of the game, check the validity of the answers by having some of the teens who signed the winner's handout perform their talent.

Conclude the activity by leading a large-group discussion of the following questions:
- What did you like about this game?
- Name some items off the handout and ask, Does _____ make someone unique and special? Why or why not?
- What makes a person original?

Complimentary Cupcakes

Large-Group Activity (15 minutes plus 10-minute break)

In this activity the teens see the connection between affirmation and self-esteem.

Before the retreat, make or buy enough cupcakes and toothpick flags so that you have one of each per person. Write one of the following compliments on each toothpick flag, or come up with compliments of your own. Stick a compliment flag in each cupcake.
- You're a great person!
- We're so glad you're here!
- You have a winning smile!
- The world's a better place because you're in it!
- We like being with you!
- You are very precious!
- Your participation is valuable!
- You can change the world!
- Thanks for being so cooperative!
- You have many gifts and talents!
- You are very special!

Inform the teens that you are going to take a break and have a snack. Tell them to save the flag that is in their cupcake.

Give the group a 10-minute break. After the break, gather the teens in a large-group circle and ask each person to read his or her compliment and then answer this question:
- When has someone said this or something similar to you before, and how did it make you feel?

After everyone has shared their compliment, ask the whole group:
- What is the connection between compliments and self-esteem?
- What is the power of compliments?

Talents Sculpture

Small-Group Activity (20–25 minutes)

In this activity the retreatants name the qualities and talents that they feel make them special.

1. Reassemble the teens in small groups. Give slips of scrap paper, markers, and masking tape to each small group. Then express the following directions in your own words:
- First discuss the various talents that the people in your small group have. Then write each of those talents on a separate slip of paper. Do

not list each talent more than once. If two or more people play basketball, for example, write "basketball" down on only one piece of paper. Then use your talent papers to make some type of structure. It can be as simple as a chain or as elaborate as a tower. When all the groups have completed their structure, they take turns explaining to the other groups their structure and the talents that make it up. Every small-group member should participate in the explanation.

This activity is meant to affirm the teens, so allow enough time for them to finish. You may need to clarify for some groups the types of talents that are appropriate for them to list. For example, some groups may feel that guzzling beer is a talent. Explain to them that a talent is something that builds up a person as well as helps other people to grow.

After all the groups are done, have them read off their talents and explain their structure to the other groups. Applaud each group after its presentation.

This activity needs little debriefing because it is meant as an affirmation. One way to end it is to simply say:

• What a talented group of teens we have here. Give yourselves another round of applause.

Self-Esteem Scramble

Small-Group Activity (10–15 minutes)

The purpose of this activity is to give the teens a definition of *self-esteem* to think about.

Ahead of time, prepare the clues for each small group. Type or write out the following definition of self-esteem for each small group: Self-esteem is loving yourself the way God loves you. Cut each definition into nine clues, one word per piece of paper. Put each set of clues in a brown lunch bag.

1. Give one bag of clues to each team. Place the teams at one end of the room and their bags at the other end. Direct the players, one at a time, to run to their team bag, grab one folded piece of paper, and return to the team with the clue. Continue until all nine clues are retrieved. Then tell the small groups to assemble the clues into the correct definition of self-esteem and signal you when they think they have the correct answer. The first small group to correctly assemble the definition is the winning team.

2. Process the activity by asking the whole group the following questions:
• How do we know God loves us?
• How do we know God accepts us for who we are?

3. Continue the discussion by sharing the following story with the whole group:
• Another way of defining self-esteem is believing in yourself even when others don't believe in you. Believing in yourself means that you believe that God has blessed you in many ways and that you are good. Let me tell you the story of one person for whom many had given up hope. Her name is Wilma Rudolph.

Can you imagine what it would be like to lose your ability to walk? That's what happened to track champion Wilma Rudolph when she was four years old. She got pneumonia, scarlet fever, and polio at the same time. She was very sick. She nearly died. Her left leg became so weak that she couldn't walk. Even though she was forced to sit in a chair, she still tried to play games with her friends. Wilma had hope, and that kept her going. She was determined that one day, somehow, she would walk again.

Fortunately for Wilma, her family loved her very much. Both her parents worked full-time with only one day off each week. On that day, Wilma's mother would drive her to the doctor in Nashville, forty-five miles away.

Wilma's brothers and sisters helped massage her leg four times a day. Very slowly Wilma became stronger. When she was six, she got a pair of special shoes. She could stand up. Finally, by age eleven, Wilma was able to walk and run on her own, without any special equipment.

She started playing basketball and made the school team. In her sophomore year she scored 803 points in twenty-five games. She was also a great runner.

At age sixteen Wilma entered the Olympics. Her relay team won a third-place bronze medal. But when Wilma ran the 200-meter dash, she didn't do well. Wilma spent the next four years training. When the 1960 Olympics arrived, Wilma entered all the track events. She won three gold medals, a new record! Her team took first place in the 400-meter relay. By herself she won the 100-meter dash and the 200-meter dash.

The world fell in love with Wilma. In Russia people called her Queen of the Olympics. In France she was called the Gazelle. And in Italy they named her the Black Pearl.

Just sixteen years before, the fastest woman on earth had been unable to walk. (Adapted from Drew, *Learning the Skills of Peacemaking,* p. 138)

4. After reading the story, lead a large-group discussion of the following questions:
• What kept Wilma Rudolph believing in herself?
• How would Wilma define the term *self-esteem?*
• Do you know others who remind you of Wilma? Who?
• What role do other people play in forming our self-esteem?
• What can we learn from Wilma Rudolph?

Lunch   (45 minutes)

Icebreakers   (15 minutes)
Choose from among the icebreakers offered in the appendix of this book, or use games of your own.

Zack and Me   Small-Group Activity (20–30 minutes)
Through this activity the teens learn that self-esteem is not defined by physical characteristics.

Before the retreat, make stars and clouds out of paper, and fasten them to the ceiling of your meeting room in no particular pattern.

1. Have the young people form small groups. Then introduce the activity in your own words:
*   You may have noticed the clouds and stars on the ceiling. For this activity each small group must devise a creative way to retrieve one cloud or star. Every member of your small group must be a part of this activity. The small group with the most original method of reaching the ceiling wins. Keep in mind the safety of the members of your group as you plan. You will have 10 minutes to discuss and practice your method. Then you will perform your method, one at a time, for the whole group.

2. After 10 minutes, call time and have the small groups take turns retrieving a cloud or star. Upon completion of the activity, take a vote with the whole group to declare a winner. Small groups cannot vote for themselves.

3. Debrief the activity with the whole group using the following questions:
*   What was easy about this activity? Why?
*   What was difficult about this activity? Why?
*   How did your group decide on its method of reaching the ceiling?
*   What obstacles did you encounter? How did you overcome those obstacles?
*   What did you like about the activity?

4. Next, introduce the Scripture reading in your own words:
*   All of us have physical limitations. Some of us may think we are too small or too large. Some of us may have physical limitations we were born with; others may have limitations received through an accident or illness, like Wilma Rudolph. Our self-esteem is not defined solely by our physical attributes. For many people, limitations actually motivate them to pursue their goals. Let's listen to a story of a man who had a physical limitation but was not stopped in pursuing his goal.
    Have a volunteer read another part of the story of Zacchaeus, from Luke 10:1–9.

5. Give each person a pencil and a copy of handout 5–B, "Zack and Me." Offer this introduction to the activity:
*   Like Zacchaeus, we are all complex individuals. We have many different qualities and experiences that shape our self-esteem. You now have an opportunity to reflect on the various aspects of Zacchaeus's self-esteem and your own self-esteem. On the left side of the handout, list the positive qualities that can be admired in Zacchaeus. On the right side, list the positive qualities people admire in you.
Allow enough time for the teens to complete their handout.

6. Continue by communicating these instructions in your own words.
*   Now you will have a chance to share your answers with the other members of your small group. The leader in each group will go first and share what he or she wrote for Zack and why he or she answered

that way. Then everyone else will share their list about Zack. The leader will continue by reading off what he or she listed for his or her own self-esteem. Everyone else will follow suit. Let's have the leader be the youngest person in the group or someone who hasn't been the leader yet.

Direct the teens to hold on to their handout for the affirmation activity near the end of the retreat.

Skits Small-Group Activity (20–30 minutes)

This activity demonstrates how one can choose to have a positive self-image.

Photocopy the skit starters on resource 5–A, "Skit Starters," cut them apart, and give one starter to each small group. Direct the groups to prepare and perform a skit based on their starter. If you have more than three small groups, give the same skit starter to more than one group. Applaud after each skit.

After all the groups have performed their skits, pose these questions for discussion:
- How did you feel as you participated in your skit? [Be sure to get lots of responses to this question.]
- How are these feelings similar to the feelings people have about their physical appearance?
- Of the three types of people represented in the skits, which would you prefer to be around? Explain.
  Conclude the activity with words such as these:
- Without answering aloud, think about which person in the skits you are most like. [Pause.] Whether we think we are ugly or beautiful, smart or dumb, God loves us just the same. It is not always easy to remember this when we have a bad hair day, make a mistake, fail a test, or get reprimanded by someone. It is at those times that we need to rebuild our self-esteem.

Rebuilding Self-Esteem Small-Group Activity (20–30 minutes)

In this activity the retreatants develop strategies to help build themselves back up when their self-esteem has been wounded.

Give each small group a packet of papers with one letter of the word *self-esteem* written in large print on each piece of paper.

Offer the teens these instructions:
- Each person in your small group gets one or two letters of the word *self-esteem*. Using the letter or letters as the beginning of a word or phrase, each person should come up with one or two ways to build up others' self-esteem. Each person should then write that word or phrase next to the letter on their paper. For example:
  Smile at everyone.
  Express your appreciation for others.
  Love yourself as God loves you.
  Forgive others.

After everyone has completed their own paper or papers, direct the small-group members to tape their sheets together, vertically if possible, spelling the word *self-esteem*. Have each group come up to the front of the room and share its answers. Hang the papers on the wall and applaud each group.

Thumbs Up!

Affirmation (15–25 minutes)
This activity shows that we are each a truly unique creation because no two people have the exact same fingerprint.

Have one ink pad per small group and some paper towels for wiping ink off thumbs. Direct the teens to form small groups and get out the handout they used in the activity "Zack and Me" (handout 5–B).

Give the following directions:

• At the bottom of your handout is an outline of a hand and the words, "The qualities that make me unique are . . ." Using the ink pad, put your thumbprint in the thumb on the handout. Use a paper towel to wipe any excess ink off your thumb. Then pass your handout around to the other members of your small group. When you receive each handout, think about the person whose thumbprint is on the paper and write down a quality or talent you appreciate in that person. Continue until you have written something on the handout of each person in your small group.

When everyone is done writing, allow enough time for them to find their own handout and read their affirmations quietly.

Wrap up the activity by communicating these ideas in your own words:

• Just as there are no two thumbprints alike, no two people are alike. God made each of us special and unique. God calls us all to share our gifts. Knowing we are gifted can boost our self-esteem, especially at times when we are feeling insignificant.

Closing Guided Meditation

(20–30 minutes)
Begin the meditation with a progressive muscle relaxation exercise (see part C of the appendix for suggestions). If possible, play soft instrumental background music. Then continue with the following guided meditation. Pause for a few seconds at each ellipsis (. . .).

• Every day you look at yourself in a mirror. Some days you are pleased with what you see, and other days you are likely disappointed. Keeping a positive self-esteem is not always easy, especially during your teenage years when so many changes are happening to you. Remember that God made you, loves you, and can give you the strength you need to become the person God created you to be.

In your mind go to your favorite room in your house—a place you like to be. Picture the colors in this room, the items that are there, . . . any smells or scents. . . . Now someone enters this room. . . . It is Jesus. . . . He is smiling because he is very happy to be with you. . . . Jesus wants to spend some time getting to know you better. . . .

Show Jesus around your favorite room. . . . Show him some of the special items that are here and why they are so special to you. [Longer pause.] Jesus smiles and nods as you explain each item. . . . Show Jesus an item that represents a time when you were really proud of yourself, and tell Jesus about that time. [Longer pause.] You can tell by the expression on Jesus' face that he is very proud of you, too. . . . Show Jesus an item that represents a person who taught you something, and tell Jesus about that person. [Longer pause.] Show Jesus the most precious gift you have ever received; tell him why that gift is so precious to you. [Longer pause.]

Jesus wants to show you one of his most precious gifts. . . . He opens up his wallet, and it's a picture of you! . . . Tell Jesus how this makes you feel. [Longer pause.]

Jesus says: "I know it is not always easy being yourself. . . . A lot of people didn't understand me when I was on earth. . . . I had to keep praying to God and reminding myself that I knew who I was and what I was called to do. . . ."

Jesus asks, "What's the hardest thing about being you, and how can I help you to appreciate yourself and to share yourself with others?" [Longer pause.]

Jesus continues: "I know you are a gift from God. . . . You are special and unique, and I love you. What is one thing that you really like about yourself?" [Longer pause.]

Jesus asks: "Who helps build up your self-esteem? . . . How does this person do that? [Longer pause.]

"Tell me about a time you helped someone else with her or his self-esteem." [Longer pause.]

Jesus inquires: "Is there anyone in particular you would like me to bless, someone who is sick or in need of guidance?" . . . Talk to Jesus about one or more people you would like him to bless. [Longer pause.]

Jesus says, "It's time for me to go now, but before I do, are there any other questions or thoughts you would like to share with me?" . . . Spend a few moments talking with Jesus or just being with him. [Longer pause.]

Jesus thanks you for spending this time with him and says, "Any time you want to be with me, go to a quiet place, and we will be together to talk again." . . .

Jesus holds your hands in his and turns your hands face up and says: "See these hands, the fingertips. . . . No one else will ever have the same fingerprint as you have. . . . Your fingerprint distinguishes you from others and makes you special. . . . Whenever you begin to doubt yourself, look at your hands and remind yourself of your uniqueness."

Jesus leaves, and this gives you an opportunity to say a prayer to Jesus: "Dear Jesus, thank you for being my best friend and for always bringing out the best in me. When I've had a discouraging day, let me remember to laugh a little and to continue to believe in myself. When I feel really good about myself, remind me to be grateful. Give me the strength to help build up other people's self-esteem rather than tear it down. Amen."

When you open your eyes, you will no longer be in your favorite room but back here in this room. When you are ready, slowly open your eyes and come back.

Evaluation (5 minutes)

After the guided meditation, invite the teens to reflect in writing on the following questions. Tell them that they may answer aloud if they feel comfortable doing so.

- If you had only one word to describe today, what word would you pick?
- What is one new thing you learned today, or what is one thing you really liked? (It could be something we did or something someone said.)
- What do you feel God is challenging you to do as a result of this retreat?

I'm an Original

B	I	N	G	O
Action: Can tap dance	Has no middle name	Has never seen *Beverly Hills 90210*	Has met a famous person	Plays a musical instrument
Is named after a movie star or other famous person	Has gone hot-air ballooning	Has more than fifteen cousins	Action: Can wiggle his or her ears	Eats broccoli
Has traveled out of the country	Has been to a Broadway play	Action: Can do ten push-ups	Has never been on a retreat before	Action: Can say "I love you" in a language other than English
Likes hot dogs with ketchup	Action: Can say the alphabet backwards	Believes in guardian angels	Has never broken a bone	Is double-jointed
Action: Can recite the Ten Commandments	Has naturally curly hair	Action: Can count from 1 to 10 forward and backward	Has moved more than five times	Is an only child

Zack and Me

In the left column, list the positive qualities you admire in Zacchaeus. In the right column, list the positive qualities people admire in you.

Zaccheus   Me _____
                                                      (name)

_____   _____

_____   _____

_____   _____

_____   _____

_____   _____

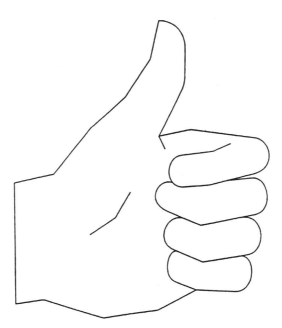

The qualities that make me unique are . . .

Skit Starters

--✂

1. *Main character.* Person with no self-esteem or very low self-esteem

   Develop a skit in which one character is always negative about himself or herself. For example, if asked to go to a pool party, this character might say, "No, I don't want anyone to see my ugly feet." Or if the character is asked to play baseball, he or she might respond, "No, I can never hit the ball, and I'd look stupid." Put this character in situations that show low self-image. Have this character blame other people, including God, for his or her inadequacies.

--✂

2. *Main character.* Person with a giant ego

   Develop a skit in which one character is stuck-up to the point of being obnoxious. For example, if asked to play tennis, this character might say: "Yeah! Nobody can beat me. I have all the right moves. They wanted me to be in the Olympics, but I said no." Put this character in a situation that really shows her or his huge ego. Have this character credit God for creating her or him better than anybody else.

--✂

3. *Main character.* Person with balanced self-esteem

   Develop a skit in which the main character recognizes his or her strengths and weaknesses and still tries to be involved. Demonstrate how a person with a balanced perspective somewhere between no self-esteem and a giant ego might respond to common situations with friends. For example, have the character respond to a friend's invitation to play a musical instrument with a band or to join in any sporting event.

--✂

Retreat 6

Sexuality

Theme
This retreat invites teens to see their sexuality as a gift from God, and it teaches them how to share that gift appropriately with others.

Bible Basis
Gen. 1:26–27,31. In Genesis we learn that God made everything, and everything is good. God's special creation is man and woman. We have been given great responsibility to share ourselves with others respectfully and with great integrity.

Objectives
The retreatants will do the following:
- distinguish between myths and truths about sexuality
- understand sexuality as a gift from God
- appreciate their own unique gift of maleness or femaleness
- explore the influence of outside forces on their understanding of sexuality
- create techniques for resisting sexual pressures

Retreat at a Glance

The following chart offers a brief overview of the retreat activities, time frames, and materials needed. For more detailed information about any of the activities, refer to the directions given in the Retreat in Detail section.

ACTIVITY	TIME FRAME	SUPPLIES
Welcome and Introduction	10–15 minutes	poster with standards
Icebreakers	15–30 minutes	depends on selection
Opening Prayer	5 minutes	Bible
Truths and Lies	10 minutes	newsprint, markers
Today's Teens	15–20 minutes	coin, newsprint, marker
Fabulous Flag	20 minutes	handout 6–A, pencils, newsprint, marker
God's Creation	15–20 minutes	paper plates
Break	10 minutes	
What's New?	20 minutes	newsprint, markers, Bibles
Male or Female?	15 minutes	
Sexuality Lecturette	10 minutes	newsprint, marker
Sex Media Search	20 minutes	poster board, notebook paper, pencils, scissors, markers, masking tape, magazines, CD ads, old posters, and other materials teens read, newsprint, marker
Lunch	45 minutes	
Icebreakers	15 minutes	depends on selection
Stealing Sex Respect	15–20 minutes	empty soft drink cans, blindfold, pen, index cards, newsprint, markers
Saying I Love You Without Sex	10–15 minutes	newsprint, markers
Resist	25–30 minutes	resource 6–A, scissors, newsprint, marker
Compliment Contest	15–20 minutes	
Closing Guided Meditation	25-30 minutes	instrumental music, tape or CD player
Evaluation	5 minutes	pencils, paper

Retreat in Detail

Welcome and Introduction   (10–15 minutes)

Icebreakers   (15–30 minutes)
Choose from among the icebreakers offered in part A of the appendix of this book, or use games of your own.

Opening Prayer   (5 minutes)
Begin the prayer by reading Gen. 1:27–28,31—the story of the creation of man and woman. Finish by offering the following prayer in your own words:
• Dear God, thank you for the goodness of your creation. We know that we humans are your special creation. We have the responsibility to respect everything you made, especially one another. Thank you for making us male and female. Help us to grow in our understanding of ourselves and one another. Teach us to share our uniqueness carefully and respectfully.

  Thank you for giving us love. Let us love one another as you have loved us. Amen.

Truths and Lies   Small-Group Activity (10 minutes)
In this activity the retreatants experience people both lying and telling the truth. The activity is designed to help the teens recognize when someone is being honest.

1. Direct the retreatants to form small groups. Write the following sentence starters on newsprint:
• My favorite TV show or movie is . . .
• My ideal vacation is . . .
• My favorite Saturday activity is . . .
• My favorite sport or hobby is . . .
Introduce the activity this way:
• Every small-group member will complete these statements, telling the truth about three of them and lying about one of them. The other group members must try and guess which item the person is lying about. The person with the shortest first name goes first.

2. After the game, lead a discussion with the whole group based on the following questions (see page 12 of the introduction for alternative ways of debriefing this and other retreat activities):
• How do you know if someone is lying?
• How do you know if someone is telling the truth?

3. In your own words, offer a conclusion like this:
• Today we will be exploring God's great gift to us: our sexuality. During the retreat we want to discover ways to distinguish the truths about sexuality from the myths about sexuality.

Today's Teens   Small-Group Activity (15–20 minutes)
The purpose of this activity is to see how the retreatants feel about the views of other teens their age.

1. Form two teams with boys and girls on each team. If you have more than twenty people, form four teams.

2. Introduce the activity with words similar to these:
*   We're going to play a guessing game about teens like you. The first five questions are taken from a survey of one hundred middle school teens who were asked about their lives. The second five questions are from a Gallup National Youth Survey for Junior High Achievement. This survey asked ten- to thirteen-year-olds how important various qualities are to their life's work.

    This is how the game is played. When I read the question, the first team decides what percentage between one and one hundred is the correct answer. A majority of the team must agree on the answer before it's given. Each team designates a speaker. Only the speaker may answer out loud. If another person does, you lose your turn. After the answer is given, the second team must guess whether the actual answer is higher or lower than the first team's answer. If the second team guesses correctly, it answers the next question first. If the second team guesses wrong, the first team answers the next question first. Each question is worth five thousand points. The final question is worth twenty thousand points. Any questions?

3. Flip a coin to determine which team goes first. Keep score on newsprint. Direct the teams to answer these questions from the first survey in a percentage between one and one hundred:
*   Out of one hundred girls surveyed, how many said their favorite Saturday activity was sleep? [62]
*   Out of one hundred boys surveyed, how many said their favorite Saturday activity was sleep? [21]
*   Out of one hundred girls surveyed, how many said the first thing they notice about a boy is his personality? [36]
*   Out of one hundred boys surveyed, how many said the first thing they notice about a girl is her looks? [93]
*   Out of one hundred participants (boys and girls) surveyed, how many said the best thing about growing up is more freedom? [39]
                (Adapted from Warden, ed., *Guys and Girls*, pp. 14–15)

    Direct the teens to answer these questions from the second survey with a percentage between one and one hundred:
*   How many young people said helping others was important to their life's work? [88 percent]
*   How many said improving their community was important? [76 percent]
*   How many said having people respect and look up to them was important? [70 percent]
*   How many said being creative was important? [54 percent]
*   How many said making a lot of money was important? [39 percent]
                (*Jr. High Ministry*, April–May 1995, p. 5)
When the game is over, declare a winner.

4. Discuss the following questions as a large group:
*   Do you disagree with any of the statistics? Which ones? Why?
*   What did you like about this game? What did you dislike?

- Which answer or statistic was most surprising to you?
- How do you feel after taking this quiz and learning this information?

5. Continue the activity with these words:
- In the game the correct answers depended on the responses of teens like you. Likewise, as we grow into adulthood we often base our thoughts about what's "normal" on the opinions of those around us. If you are a boy and boys around you say girls are "gross," you might agree. Or if you are a girl and girls around you say some boys are "so immature," you might agree.

6. Next, ask these questions:
- Did the survey answers reflect your opinions and interests? Explain.
- How are your present opinions and interests similar to the opinions and interests you had as a child?
- How are your present opinions and interests different from your childhood opinions and interests?

7. Conclude the activity by expressing the following thoughts in your own words:
- When you compare the things that interested you as a child with the things that interest you now, you can see how much you've changed. One thing that may have changed is how you feel about the other sex. As you grow older, you need to learn to relate to, and communicate with, one another. We can learn how to do that by understanding how girls and boys each respond to issues of growing up.

Fabulous Flag   **Individual Activity and Paired Exchange (20 minutes)**
In this activity the retreatants learn to appreciate their uniqueness.

1. Have the teens spread out so that no one is close to anyone else. Give each person a copy of handout 6–A, "Fabulous Flag," and a pencil. List the instructions on newsprint, and communicate them verbally also:
- Complete the handout by writing your name in the top border of the flag and drawing one picture in each section of the flag, according to these instructions:
   ○ *Top left.* A gift I treasure
   ○ *Top center.* What I do best
   ○ *Top right.* A time I was really proud of myself
   ○ *Bottom left.* One goal for my future
   ○ *Bottom center.* One thing I'd like to change about myself
   ○ *Bottom right.* Best thing about being male (if male) or female (if female)

2. When the young people are finished, direct them to find a partner of the other sex. If your male-female ratio is uneven, allow same-sex partnerships. Encourage the partners to briefly share their completed handouts.

3. Next, raise these questions to the whole group for discussion:
- Did you learn anything new about yourself? about your partner?
- Why is it important to think about and talk about these aspects of life?

4. List on newsprint the things they wrote for what's best about being male or female. Ask if anyone wants to add other qualities to the lists. Leave these posted so that you can refer back to them during the sexuality lecturette, which comes later in the retreat.

5. Offer this conclusion in your own words:
- As we can see from these fabulous flags, both boys and girls have goals and God-given strengths that will help them grow and mature into adulthood. By recognizing one another's goals and strengths, we can learn to respect one another for who we are rather than for what sex we happen to be.

God's Creation

Small-Group Activity (15–20 minutes)

This activity reminds the teens that God made everything and that humans are his special creation.

1. Form the teens into small groups. Give each person a paper plate. Explain these instructions:
- Think of some of the great things God has created—things that you are grateful you have been given. Using only your paper plate, shape it into one of the things God created. This is to be done in silence.

2. After the teens have completed their project, say:
- Each person will have a chance to explain what her or his creation is, but first the other members in the small group must try and guess what each person created. Let's have the person with the smallest shoe size show her or his creation first.

3. When the guessing and explaining are finished, lead a large-group discussion of the following questions:
- How many created nonliving things?
- How many created something from nature?
- How many created an animal?
- How many created human beings?
- How many created something other than the items I've mentioned?

4. Conclude the activity this way:
- In the Scriptures we learn that God created everything and declared it good, and that the greatest creation was us. God created male and female because God did not want man or woman to be alone. God wanted us to be cocreators in the continuation of human life.

Break (10 minutes)

What's New?

Small-Group Activity (20 minutes)

This activity ensures that the retreatants have the correct information about the changes that occur during puberty.

1. Form two groups: boys in one, girls in the other. It's okay if the two groups are uneven in size. Give each group some newsprint and markers.

2. Introduce the activity by expressing the following thoughts in your own words:

- Let's look at the changes our bodies go through during puberty. Each small group is to list on newsprint all the physical changes that take place in the other sex during puberty. Be as honest as you can. For this exercise you will need a recorder, who will write the changes on the newsprint, and a reporter, who will read the group's list aloud. Let's have the recorder be the youngest person in the group, and the reporter be the oldest person in the group. Any questions?

   This may be an uncomfortable assignment for some junior high students, but they can work through it with encouragement and guidance. Let them know that you think they can handle the exercise with maturity. Still, expect some giggling and secretiveness.

3. After a few minutes, invite the groups to share their lists with each other. Use the following lists to correct any misinformation. Make sure that these items are part of the groups' lists:

Male Changes	*Female Changes*
Grow to full height	Grow to full height
Body hair grows	Body hair grows
Skin gets oilier (acne may strike)	Skin gets oilier (acne may strike)
Reproductive organs grow	Breasts grow
Voice deepens	Menstruation begins
Sexual desires increase	Sexual desires increase
Emotions shift rapidly	Emotions shift rapidly

4. Spark a discussion with the whole group by asking these questions:
- Girls, what surprised you about what the boys listed as female changes?
- Boys, what surprised you about what the girls listed as male changes?
- How did you feel as you made the lists and talked about them?
- What made this activity uncomfortable for you?
- How is this uncomfortable feeling similar to the way we feel about the changes in boys' and girls' bodies?

5. Continue the activity by saying something like the following:
- Talking about our bodies is sometimes embarrassing. But in Song of Songs, King Solomon praises the human body. He saw no shame in the beauty of our bodies, which are created by God.

Distribute a Bible to each group. Have the boys read Song of Songs 4:1–7, and the girls read Song of Songs 5:10–16.

6. After the teens have read their Scripture passage within their group, direct them to form one large circle. Then raise this question:
- How did this passage make you feel? Make a facial expression to indicate your feelings. [Pause.] You may have been happy, surprised, upset, or confused. Hold your facial expression for a minute and look around at others' expressions.

Continue by asking these questions:
- How are the responses people had to the Scripture passage similar? How are they different?

7. Have one boy and one girl summarize the passages they read. Make sure they know that Song of Songs 4:1–7 is a description of a beautiful woman, and Song of Songs 5:10–16 is a description of a handsome man.

8. Then pose the following questions for discussion:
- What were you thinking as you read your Song of Songs passage?
- What's the difference between these passages and the way the media portray the human body?
- What can we learn about our bodies from these Scripture passages?
- What can we learn about our feelings toward the other sex from these Scripture passages?
- What are some of the similar responses boys and girls have to the physical changes they're going through in puberty?
- How have your feelings about the other sex changed in the past year or two?

9. Conclude the activity in your own words:
- Our sexuality is part of God's plan for us. Puberty can be a difficult step on the road to maturity, but as a growth and transition step, it can be a time of hope and anticipation.

(Adapted from Warden, ed., *Guys and Girls,* pp. 24–26)

Male or Female?   Large-Group Activity (15 minutes)

This activity identifies stereotypes about male and female roles.

Designate one side of the room as "Male Roles," the other side as "Female Roles," and the middle of the room as "Both Male and Female Roles."

Read the roles, one at a time, from the following list. After each role is read, direct the teens to respond by standing near the sign that best represents their belief as to whether the role is male-oriented, female-oriented, or both.
- secretary
- lawyer
- police officer
- cooking meals
- fixing a leaky faucet
- doing housework
- paying for a date
- taking care of children
- being realistic
- shopping for groceries
- buying a car
- remembering important dates

When all teens have made their decision about a role, invite volunteers to explain why they chose as they did. Continue in this fashion until all the roles have been read or time is expired.

Pose these questions for discussion:
- Do boys and girls have different ideas about gender roles? Why or why not?
- How does our society tell us what is a male role and what is a female role?

- How do you feel when you do a job that's considered part of the other sex's role?
- Is it important to have different roles for males and females?
- What is a stereotype?
- What are some roles that in the past were seen only as male roles? as female roles?

  Conclude the activity with this summary:
- Stereotypes are prevalent in our society today. A stereotype is a generalization. When we generalize we don't treat people as unique individuals. Therefore, a stereotype can be limiting and even false. We know that God has created us as special and unique individuals. Therefore, we are free to choose our roles. Many people in our society have broken through stereotypes. Overcoming stereotypes can allow us to become the people God created us to be.

Sexuality Lecturette

Large-Group Activity (10 minutes)

The purpose of this activity is to pull together the important points of the morning and to present a working definition of the word *sexuality*.

Brainstorm with the group what the word *sexuality* means based on the activities done thus far. Be sure to refer to the list of best qualities of each gender gathered from the Fabulous Flag activity carried out earlier. List the young people's answers on newsprint. Correct any misinformation.

Supplement their answers with the following ideas:
- Understanding the concept of sexuality is a complicated and, at times, confusing task. To put it simply, sexuality is understanding who we are. We learn about who we are from a variety of places. Some sources that lead us to a deeper understanding of who we are include the Scriptures, the church, the society we live in, our peer group, and our family. As we grow in knowledge of who we are, we grow closer to God. God created both men and women, therefore the sexes are equally important. Each person brings his or her own specialness to the world. We are called to respect our own gift of sexuality as well as the sexuality of other people.

  Conclude the activity by asking the whole group:
- What are some specific ways we can respect our own sexuality and the sexuality of others?

Sex Media Search

Small-Group Activity (20 minutes)

This activity highlights the powerful influence the media have on forming our ideas about sexuality.

1. Form small groups. Give each small group a piece of poster board, a scissors, markers, masking tape, magazines, CD ads, old posters, tabloids, and anything else the retreatants read regularly.

   Explain these instructions:
- Search your materials for messages about sex. They can be true or false. Cut out the words and pictures and tape them onto your poster board. Find as many messages as you can. Add messages not found in your materials—ones you've heard from friends at school, or on favorite TV shows and videos.

2. When the groups are finished, have each one explain its poster. Applaud after each presentation.

3. Next, direct each small group to pass its poster to the small group to its left. Give each small group two pieces of notebook paper. Explain these instructions:
- Scan each poster for truths and myths. Write myths on one page and truths on the other. For this you will need a recorder and a reporter. Let's have the recorder be the person with the shortest hair, and the reporter be the person with the longest hair. After you finish with one poster, pass it to the left and begin working on the next poster. Continue working until you have recorded the myths and truths from every poster. Any questions?

4. After 5 minutes, call for the small groups to tape their posters and papers to the wall. Invite volunteers to point out the most important truths and the most believed myths. Discuss these questions with the group as a whole:
- Why is it important to pinpoint myths?
- What makes it easy or hard to believe the truths?

    After several responses have been offered, use the retreatants' words to write on a sheet of newsprint a statement similar to this one:
- Believing myths about sex or failing to understand truths about sex causes unhappiness. The best source of truth is the Creator of sexuality, God. God has created each of you as a sexual and lovable person.

    (Adapted from Dockrey, *Jr. High Retreats and Lock-Ins,* pp. 93–95)

Lunch (45 minutes)

Icebreakers (15 minutes)
Choose from among the icebreakers offered in part A of the appendix of this book, or use games of your own.

Stealing Sex Respect Large-Group Activity (15–20 minutes)
This activity helps the retreatants to recognize things that show disrespect for the gift of our sexuality and to discover ways to avoid or overcome them.

    Before the retreat, write each one of the following on a separate 3-by-5-inch index card:
- pornography
- premarital sex
- television
- peer pressure
- rebellion
- low self-esteem
- physical drives
- curiosity
- the need to belong
- the need for intimacy or love

1. Have the teens sit in a circle on the floor. Ask for a volunteer to be the "keeper of the sex respect." Direct the keeper to sit blindfolded in the center of the circle. Place six soft-drink cans within easy reach of the keeper. Give the keeper an opportunity to feel the cans and know their exact location.

2. Explain these instructions:
• These cans represent sex respect, and the keeper must prevent the sex respect from being stolen. If anyone tries to steal the sex respect and is touched by the keeper, that "thief" is rendered powerless for the rest of the game. The keeper must remain seated but can do anything except cover or hold the cans to protect them.

3. Give one card each to ten young people. Convey these directions to them in your own words:
• The items written on these cards can be thieves of sex respect. One person at a time will call out the item on their card and then try to steal a sex respect can without being touched by the keeper.
  When all the cans have been stolen, or all the items on the cards called out, enlist another keeper, return the cans to the center of the circle, and play again.

4. Lead a discussion with the whole group based on the following questions:
• Thieves, how did you feel as you tried to steal the sex respect?
• Keepers, how did you feel when you knew someone was trying to steal something you were supposed to protect? How did you feel when they were unsuccessful? successful?
• Audience, how did you feel as you watched other people try to steal the sex respect?
• What would have made it impossible for the thieves to steal the sex respect?

5. Next, have the teens break into small groups. Give each group one of the index cards and a marker. Say something like this:
• In your small group discuss the following questions. You need another recorder and reporter. Let's have two people that haven't been picked yet do it.
  Write these questions on newsprint:
• How does this item rob us of sex respect?
• What can we do to prevent it from stealing our sex respect?

6. When the groups are finished, have the reporters share their answers with the other groups.
  (Adapted from Jamie Snodgrass, "Sex Respect," *Jr. High Ministry*, September–October 1991, pp. 36–37. Reprinted by permission from *Jr. High Ministry* Magazine, copyright © 1991 by Group Publishing, P.O. Box 481, Loveland, CO 80539.)

Saying I Love You Without Sex   Small-Group Activity (10–15 minutes)
This activity helps the retreatants develop healthy, nonsexual ways of expressing love to other people.

Form small groups. Give each small group a piece of newsprint and a marker. Say something like this:

- There are many ways to say "I love you" besides having sex. Creative ways of expressing love show the other person that you took the time to think about him or her and plan something special. You will have 5 minutes to write on your newsprint as many ways as possible. You will need a group recorder to write the things down and a group reporter to read them off. Let's have the recorder be the person whose first letter of their last name is closest to the beginning of the alphabet, and the reporter be the person whose first letter of their last name is closest to the end of the alphabet.

  I'll give you the first one: do homework together. [Other examples: give or get a hug, make the other person feel important and respected, find out what's special for the other person and do it, tell the other person you care, walk arm in arm, play footsie, make each other gifts.]

  After 5 minutes, call time. Have each reporter read off its group's list and count the items. Let everyone know which group had the longest list.

Resist Small-Group Activity (25–30 minutes)

In this activity the retreatants create verbal and physical techniques to resist sexual pressure.

Before the retreat, photocopy resource 6–A, "Role-Play Starters," cut it apart on the dashed lines, and distribute one starter to each small group. If you have more than five groups, give the same starter to more than one group.

1. Introduce the activity this way:
- Each small group will be given the beginning of a role-play about someone who is being pressured into having sex. The group's job is to finish the role-play by dramatizing both verbal and physical techniques the pressured person can use to say no. These techniques must be healthy and nonviolent. Everyone in your small group must participate in the role-play. Each small group will perform its role-play for the whole group. After each role-play has been presented, the observing groups will try to guess which resistance techniques the group employed.

Give the groups time to prepare their role-plays.

2. After each small group has presented its role-play, ask the observing groups to share aloud the techniques they saw the presenting group employ. Write these down on a sheet of newsprint. Continue in this fashion until all the small groups have presented their role-play.

3. To conclude this activity, review the newsprint list of resistance techniques. Make any corrections as necessary. Ask the group if any techniques were forgotten and, if so, add them as well.

4. Finish by offering this conclusion:
- We do not have to give in to sexual pressure. We have many resistance techniques to choose from. Today we discovered many that we can use if we are confronted with the pressure to have sex.

Compliment Contest

Affirmation (15–20 minutes)

This activity allows the retreatants to pick the people whom they want to affirm them.

Have everyone, including adults, sit in a circle. Choose a person to be "It." "It" sits in the circle's center and chooses two people to give her or him a compliment. "It" picks his or her favorite compliment of the two, and that complimenter then becomes "It." Each new "It" must choose two complimenters who have not yet been chosen. Do this until each person has been chosen at least once and each person has had a chance to be "It."

(Wendy Lewis, "How to Connect with Kids," *Jr. High Ministry,*
April–May 1992, p. 14. Reprinted by permission from
Jr. High Ministry Magazine, copyright © 1992 by Group Publishing,
P.O. Box 481, Loveland, CO 80539.)

Closing Guided Meditation

(25–30 minutes)

Begin the meditation with a progressive muscle relaxation exercise (see part C of the appendix for suggestions). If possible, play soft instrumental background music. Then continue with the following guided meditation. Pause for a few seconds at each ellipsis (. . .).

• In the Scriptures we learn that God created everything. The greatest creation is us. God created different species and genders because God wanted complementary relationships to be sources of joy and fulfillment, and God wanted to allow created beings to participate in the continuation of life.

The Scriptures also tell us that everything God made is good. Unfortunately people sometimes take good things and twist them around for evil purposes. Our body and our sexuality are special gifts God has made, and God wants us to use them to honor God and one another.

Imagine yourself getting up out of your body and leaving this room. You step out onto a beautiful sandy beach. . . . You're the only one here. . . . You're not afraid; it's very peaceful. . . . It's a beautiful day . . . the weather is warm and sunny . . . the sky is blue with a few puffy white clouds. . . . Every once in a while birds fly overhead. . . . You walk up to the shore, . . . bend down, and put your hands into the clear, warm water. . . .

Now you notice someone at a distance on the beach. . . . This person is walking toward you. . . . As the person gets closer, you recognize him. . . . It's Jesus. . . . He's come to spend some time with you. . . . What does Jesus look like? . . . How tall is he? . . . What is he wearing? . . . What color are his eyes? . . . his skin tone? . . . his hair? . . . You notice that he's smiling, . . . indicating that he is happy you've taken the time to be with him. . . .

Now Jesus is right up next to you and greets you by saying your name. . . . He invites you to sit down with him on the beach for a while. . . . Jesus says: "Growing up isn't always easy. . . . There are so many changes that go on . . . some things we don't understand. . . . But I understand. . . . I was young like you and went through all the things you are experiencing right now." . . .

The way Jesus looks at you makes you believe him. . . . You feel that you can tell him anything and he won't judge you or reject you. . . . He loves you for who you are right now. . . . Jesus asks you, "What are some of your concerns about growing up?" . . . Spend a few moments sharing with Jesus and hearing him answer you. [Longer pause.]

Jesus continues, "What are some of the things about growing up that you like and enjoy?" [Longer pause.]

Jesus goes on and asks, "What's one new skill or talent you have learned recently?" [Longer pause.] Jesus says: "That's one great thing about growing up. . . . We learn so many new things, . . . and we become fuller human beings. . . . What else do you like about yourself?" [Longer pause.]

Jesus reassures you: "Growing up can be scary if we try to do it all alone. . . . You are never alone. . . . I am always with you. . . . In case you didn't know . . . I want to be your best friend. . . . Come and talk to me any time. . . .

"I know there are people you trust . . . people you turn to for understanding and advice. . . . Tell me about some of these special people and what they have done for you." [Longer pause.]

Jesus says, "Before I go is there anything else you want to talk to me about?" Spend these last few minutes sharing with Jesus or just being silent and enjoying his company. [Longer pause.]

Jesus says that it's time for him to go now. . . . The two of you stand up, and Jesus begins to give you a sign of his love and friendship. . . . It might be a handshake, a hug, a pat on the back, a high five, or a special greeting. . . . Feel Jesus now give you that sign of love and friendship. [Longer pause.] Now Jesus turns and walks back down the beach away from you. . . . The further he walks, the smaller and smaller he appears. . . . Now you can no longer see him . . . but you feel his presence . . . right beside you, giving you strength and peace. . . .

So you sit back down on the beach, . . . close your eyes, . . . and say a little prayer: "Jesus, thank you for spending this time with me and for letting me share with you my concerns and joys about growing up. So much is happening to me at this stage of my life. Help me to enjoy the great and awesome changes happening to me, and support me during the difficult and sometimes awkward stages. Let me always respect myself and others as I share myself with them. Amen."

When you open your eyes, you will no longer be on the beach but back here in this room. When you are ready, slowly open your eyes and come back.

Evaluation   **Large Group (5 minutes)**

After the guided meditation, invite the teens to reflect in writing on the following questions. Tell them that they may answer aloud if they feel comfortable doing so.

• If you had only one word to describe today, what word would you pick?

- What is one new thing you learned today, or what is one thing you really liked? (It could be something we did or something someone said.)
- What do you feel God is challenging you to do as a result of this retreat?

Fabulous Flag

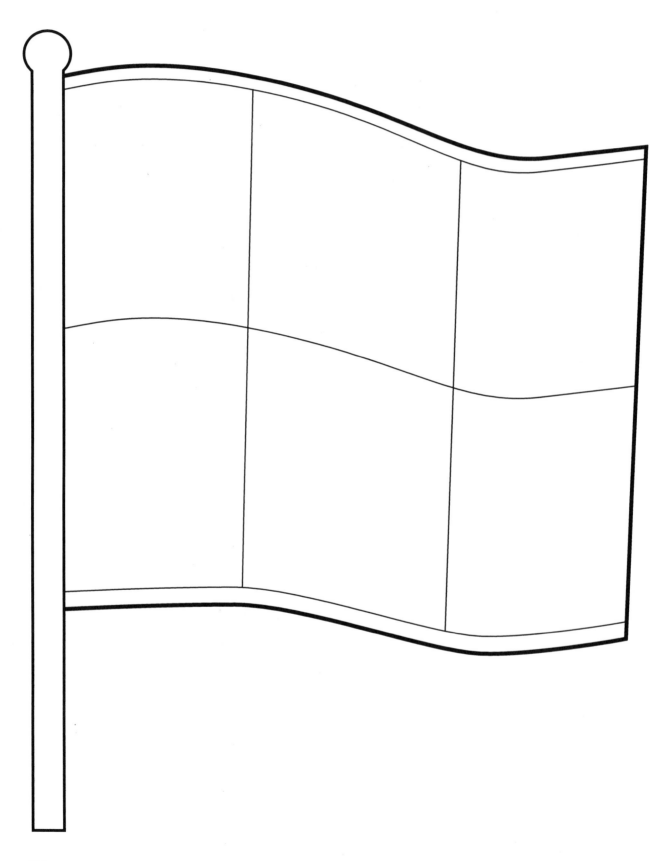

Handout 6–A: Permission to reproduce this handout for use in your program is granted.

Role-Play Starters

--- ✂

Scene 1. It's Friday night, and the high school dance is drawing to a close. During the last slow dance of the evening, Jamie says to Lucrecia, "Let's go outside to my brother's car so that we can end this evening in a special way."

Lucrecia responds, "Do you mean what I think you mean?"

Jamie answers: "I want to be alone with you. Don't be nervous, it's okay as long as we love each other."

Build into the role-play several different responses to this situation that would help Lucrecia to resist sexual pressure.

--- ✂

Scene 2. It's Saturday afternoon, and Bridget has invited Milton to her house to study for an upcoming exam. When Milton arrives, he discovers to his surprise that Bridget's parents are away. Bridget says, "I've been waiting a long time for my parents to leave me home alone so that I could have you over. Milton, I love you. I've been longing for you."

Milton responds, "I like you, too."

Bridget says, "Milton, it has hurt so much not to be able to make love to you."

Build into the role-play several different responses to this situation that would help Milton to resist sexual pressure.

--- ✂

Scene 3. It's Thursday after school, and Kim and Chuck are roller blading in the park. Chuck invites Kim to take a rest on a nearby bench.

Chuck says: "What happened to you the other night? It was great being with you. I thought you wanted to make love to me."

Kim responds: "I didn't know what your intention was."

Chuck says, "It's been my intention to make love to you for a while now. Let's go over there in that isolated spot behind the bushes."

Kim responds, "I don't think so."

Chuck retorts, "You're so selfish not to do this for me."

Build into the role-play several different responses to this situation that would help Kim to resist sexual pressure.

--- ✂

--- ✂

Scene 4. It's Friday night, and Teri and Fred have just finished watching a movie at a local theater. As they are walking home together, Teri says, "Fred, I always enjoy being with you. I've never had so much fun with anyone else. You are very special to me."

Fred responds, "Thank you, Teri, I really have a great time when we're together."

Teri continues: "Fred, I want to get even closer to you. It's okay; I've brought birth control with me."

Build into the role-play several different responses to this situation that would help Fred to resist sexual pressure.

--- ✂

Scene 5. It's a summertime evening, and Jasmine and Nikko are at an outdoor party at Nikko's house. Nikko asks Jasmine to come help him get refreshments. Once inside, Nikko says: "Jasmine, you look really great tonight. You are the most beautiful girl here. I'm so lucky you're my girl-friend."

Jasmine responds, "Thank you, Nikko. I'm so lucky you're my boy-friend."

Nikko continues, "I've planned a really special surprise for you. Let's go into the bedroom so I can show you how much I love you."

Build into the role-play several different responses to this situation that would help Jasmine to resist sexual pressure.

--- ✂

Appendix

Part A   Icebreakers

Large-Group Games

Back to Back

Direct everyone to pair off and sit on the floor, back to back. Next, tell them to lock arms and try to stand up together at the same time.

Then have each pair join with another pair and try it again with all four people sitting back to back. When these groups have been successful at standing up, combine larger and larger groups until the entire group is all in one big circle trying to stand up together in the locked-arm, back-to-back position.

(Adapted from Rice, *Up Close and Personal*, p. 32)

Bob! Bob! Bob!

Have everyone sit in a circle, with the leader standing up in the middle. The leader moves around the circle, randomly pointing at different people. When the leader points at a particular person, the rest of the group should chant that person's name loudly and in rhythm, for example, "Bob! Bob! Bob!" The leader keeps the momentum going by pointing rapidly from one person to another until everyone has been pointed to at least once. The group chants as loudly as possible and claps their hands in time.

(Adapted from Rice, *Up Close and Personal*, p. 34)

Common Matches

Before the game, write each of the following words on a separate index card:

- Adam
- Eve
- cats
- dogs
- east
- west
- up
- down
- ham
- eggs
- over
- under
- sweet
- sour
- salt
- pepper

Give each person one index card. Make sure there is a match for each person or thing named on a card—for example, Adam and Eve.

When you are ready, invite the teens to mingle around the room and find their "match." When they find that person, have them introduce themselves and wait for further instructions.

After everyone has found their mate, give each pair some scrap paper and a pencil. Tell them they will have 3 minutes to find out and write down things they have in common with their partner (they cannot use such obvious things as two arms, two eyes). They should come up with as many items as possible.

After 3 minutes, go around to each pair and have them share one thing (preferably the most unusual) they have in common.

Group Up

The entire group mingles around the room, and the leader yells out a characteristic, such as "First initial of first name." Everyone must quickly get into groups that share that characteristic (for example, Geri and George would group up). The leader then blows the whistle and identifies the group with the most people in it.

Here are some possible characteristics to use:
- number of people in your immediate family
- month of birth
- favorite color
- color of shirt
- age
- grade in school
- community you live in

(Adapted from Rice and Yaconelli, *Play It!* p. 146)

Lap Game

Direct everyone to stand in a circle shoulder to shoulder, facing in. Next, have them turn to their right, so that they are all facing the same direction. Everyone should be about six inches apart.

On the count of three, tell everyone to sit down gently on the lap of the person behind them. If your group members are really good, they should be able to walk around in a circle while sitting on laps.

(Adapted from LeFevre, *New Games for the Whole Family*, p. 131)

Line Up

Draw two parallel lines on the floor that are about 12 inches apart. Have the whole group line up between the two lines, avoiding standing on the lines.

The object of the game is to reverse the order the teens are standing in *without anyone stepping outside the lines*. It's tough to do without falling, and requires a great deal of cooperation and hanging on to one another.

Next, have the group line up according to birth date, height, or any classification, and the same rules apply. If you have more than one group participating, direct them to compete to see which group can accomplish the switch in the shortest time.

Here is a variation of the game: Line the groups up on a low wall, curb, log, or plank and tell them that the objective is to rearrange the group's order without stepping off the object.

(Adapted from Rice, *Up Close and Personal,* p. 67)

People Upset

The entire group sits in a circle with one less chair than there are people. The extra person stands in the middle. The person in the middle begins by calling out an item or quality that describes people, such as "everyone wearing the color blue." The people who have that characteristic must change chairs with one another. At the same time, the person in the middle also tries to sit down in one of the vacant chairs. The person who fails to secure a chair to sit in is then the caller for the next item or quality. If the person in the center wants everyone to get up, he or she calls out loudly, "People upset," and everyone must move.

Here are the only two rules:
- You can't sit in the chair of the person next to you.
- No diving for chairs is allowed; safety first!

Shared Musical Chairs

This game is played like regular musical chairs except that only a chair is taken away after each round, never a person. The group then has to make sure everyone has a place to sit. The fun and creativity really happens when the number of chairs gets down to three, two, and then one!

Shuffle the Deck

Distribute a playing card to each person. Then call out different combinations, like these:
- Get in a group that adds up to fifty-eight.
- Find three people of the same suit.
- Find five numbers in a row, of any suit.
- Find your whole suit.
- Find four of a kind—four 3s, four 8s, and so on

Direct the teens to form groups based on the combination called. Repeat this several times so that the teens get to meet many people. For larger groups, use multiple decks of cards; for smaller groups, don't use the whole deck. Then create your own combinations.

(Adapted from Rice, *Up Close and Personal,* p. 83)

Virginia Reel

Set up the room before the activity as follows: Place chairs in two rows facing each other. The chairs should be about 18 inches apart. When the teens enter the room, have them sit in any chair. Then give these directions:
- In front of you is your first partner. I will read an open-ended statement and give everyone 1 minute to share their answer with their partner. Then I will say "Rotate," and everyone will then move one chair to the right, facing a new partner. I will then read a new statement for each person to complete.

Here are some possible statements to use (feel free to add your own):

- My favorite color (TV show, movie, book, actor, food, music, animal, season, holiday) is . . . because . . .
- If I could be someone else in my family, I would be . . .
- If I could marry someone famous, I would marry . . .
- If I could invent something, I would invent . . .
- When I have free time, I like to . . .
- Some things I enjoy doing with friends are . . .
- Some things I enjoy doing by myself are . . .
- The world problem I am most concerned about is . . .
- The qualities I look for in a friend are . . .
- Three words that describe me are . . .
- If I could leave anything in my will to my friends, I would leave . . .
- I think the most difficult thing Christ told us to do is . . .
- For breakfast I usually . . .
- The most beautiful thing that I have ever seen is . . .
- A person who's taught me a lot is . . . because . . .
- A time I felt proud was . . .
- A birthday or holiday I'll always remember is . . .

Small-Group Games

Backward Letter Scramble

Ahead of time, make four sets of cards (one set per team), each set containing one of each of the letters *B, A, C, K, W, A, R,* and *D.*

Pass out the cards and have each team member hold one or more cards, depending on how many members are on each team.

Call out a word made up of letters from the cards (for example, card, raw, bark, crab). Direct the players holding the needed letters to line up with their letters, spelling the named word backward. The first team to do so wins.

(Adapted from Rice and Yaconelli, comps.,
Creative Activities for Small Youth Groups, pp. 81–82)

Balloons and Backs

You will need two chairs. Form two teams. Tell the retreatants on each team to divide into trios. If there's an uneven number of people, then some people will have to go twice to even out the trios.

Give each team a balloon and say:

- Stand back to back and lock arms with the other members of your trio.

Place the balloon between their backs and say:

- You must get to the chair at the other end of the room and back without the balloon getting away. Then pass the balloon to the next trio, and the race continues. If the balloon escapes, your team is out of the race. The first team finished wins.

(Adapted from Mike Gillespie, *Jr. High Ministry,* February–March 1996,
"Bountiful Balloon Fun," p. 28. Reprinted by permission from
Jr. High Ministry Magazine, copyright © 1996 by Group Publishing,
P.O. Box 481, Loveland, CO 80539.)

Body Balloon Burst

Secretly and randomly assign each person one of these body parts: right hand, left hand, right foot, left foot, mouth, rear end. There is a corresponding motion for each part of the body:

- "Right hands" raise and wave their right hands.
- "Left hands" raise and wave their left hands.
- "Right feet" hop on their right feet.
- "Left feet" hop on their left feet.
- "Mouths" yell.
- "Rear ends" do the Twist.

When the signal to go is given, each person performs the motion for his or her part of the body in an attempt to attract other body parts and form a complete, six-person "body." No other talking is allowed during this part of the game. Each body must include all six body parts.

When the body is together, the two feet carry one of the hands to the leader, who gives the hand a balloon. The hand (still being carried by the feet) takes the balloon back to its body group where the mouth must blow up the balloon. But the mouth cannot touch it—the hands must hold it for the mouth. After the mouth blows it up, the hands tie it and place it on a chair—at which time the rear end sits on it and pops it. The first team to pop its balloon is the winner.

(Adapted from Rice, *Up Close and Personal,* p. 34)

Connect-a-Name

You will need pieces of newsprint and magic markers. Form teams of four to six people each. For round one, direct the teams, when you give the signal, to each attempt to connect every team member's first name in one crossword puzzle (see diagram below) in the shortest amount of time. Give the signal "Go" for them to begin.

For round two, combine two teams and play again. Continue playing rounds until all players are in one big team making a crossword puzzle of all the names. Display the final crossword during a Bible study on 1 Corinthians, chapter 12, to illustrate that all Christians are part of the same body.

```
    K Y L E
    E
  E V A
    I
    N E L L I E
```

(Adapted from Rice and Yaconelli, *Play It Again!* p. 168)

Knots

If your group is larger than ten, divide into groups of ten or fewer. Each group stands in a circle, and all group members grab one another's hands in the center so that there is a knot of hands at the hub of each circle. Both right and left hands should be connected with someone else.

The two rules are these:

1. You cannot hold hands with the person standing to your right or left.
2. You cannot connect both your hands with the same person.

The object of the game is to untangle the knot without letting go of hands—that is, to unravel arms so that group members end up still in a circle, but holding hands with people to the left and right of them, not in a knot in the middle. Grips can be adjusted, but no letting go.

(Adapted from Rice, *Up Close and Personal,* pp. 64–65)

Kooky Kickball

Like regular kickball, one team is up to bat and the other is in the field.

The first batter kicks the ball as it is rolled to him or her by the other team. A miss, foul, or ball caught in the air is an out. There are three outs per team per inning. If no outs are made, everyone on the team may go up once during the inning. Then the other team goes up to bat.

When the ball is kicked, the fielding team lines up behind the fielder who retrieved the ball. The ball is passed between the legs of all players from front to back. The last team member then takes the ball and tags the runner.

Meanwhile, the kickers (batters) do not run around the bases. Instead, the team that is up to bat lines up single file behind the batter, who runs around the team as many times as possible. One run is scored for every complete revolution before the batter is tagged with the ball.

(Adapted from Rice and Yaconelli, *Play It!* p. 29)

Labels

This game is a form of charades. Everyone in the small group gets a label taped on their back. One at a time, everyone shows their back to the other members of their small group, who have to act out what's on the person's back until he or she guesses correctly. Then the next person in the small group goes. The pattern continues until everyone has gone.

Here are some possible suggestions for labels: Christmas, horse, doctor, baseball, guitar, surfboard, monkey, skateboard, kitten, Fourth of July, merry-go-round, dentist, alligator, football, piano, roller coaster, bicycle, dog, basketball, Thanksgiving, secretary, drums, car, eye doctor, tennis, fish, Easter, trumpet, train, Saint Patrick's Day, Ping-Pong, vacuum cleaner, elephant, teapot, toaster, clock, blender, spaghetti, cook, soccer, tuba, soup, rabbit, volleyball, harp, carpenter, pizza, Valentine's Day, hamburger, dragon, popcorn, hockey, water, Easter egg, Christmas tree, bear, computer, clown, principal, God, church, Bible, giraffe, mechanic, Santa Claus, pancakes, Nintendo.

Name Anagram

On scrap paper, have one person write each group member's first name across the top of the page. Using only those letters, the group must come up with as many words of three letters or more that they can. The team with the most number of words wins.

Popcorn

Prepare bags of popcorn ahead of time. Give one bag to each small group. Invite everyone to take as much popcorn as they want, but tell them not to eat it until instructed.

When everyone has their popcorn, explain, "For each piece of popcorn you took, you have to say one thing about yourself." More than likely the teens will have a pile of popcorn in their lap, and therefore the retreatants will learn a lot about one another.

Shoe Shuffle

If you're a jigsaw puzzle fan, you will love this one. The teens will assemble giant puzzles with their feet. You will need four large sheets of heavy-duty corrugated cardboard, two yards of wide elastic, and a utility knife. (We used a 4-by-8-foot piece of plywood and cord.)

Cut each sheet of cardboard into eight (we did sixteen) jigsaw puzzle pieces approximately 1-foot square. Punch two holes 4 inches apart in the center of each puzzle piece. Thread a piece of elastic through the holes to make a handle, tying a knot on each end to keep it from slipping through the holes.

Divide the teens into four small groups. Give each small group the puzzle pieces for one full puzzle. Be sure that each teen has one or two puzzle pieces. Ask the teens to strap the puzzle piece or pieces to their feet. Then instruct each small group to assemble its puzzle on the floor, using only their feet. No hands are allowed. Tell them that they may begin when you give the signal. Then shout "Go." The first team to construct its puzzle wins.

Scavenger Hunt Relay

Form the retreatants into small groups. Have each small group choose a "runner" for this activity. Ask everyone to get out their purse or wallet. Instruct the whole group by saying something like this:

• I am on a scavenger hunt and need many different items. Some of these items you may have in your purse or wallet. In a moment I will call out the item I need. You must then give the item called for to your runner, who must bring it to me. The first runner to reach me will score one point for his or her team.

Here is a list of items you may want to request: a penny, a stamp, a driver's license, a calendar, a stick of gum, a picture of a relative, a Band-Aid, a rubber band, matches, a key, a letter, a student ID card, a comb, a pin, a nail file, a hair scrunchie or barrette, a shoelace, a ring, a watch, a social security card, a library card, lip balm or lipstick, jewelry, a sock, sunglasses, exactly forty-one cents, a name tag, an unused tissue.

Short Fuse

You will need one pair of *huge* boxer shorts for every team of three to six young people. You can make them by folding an old sheet in half, cutting it in half, cutting out the legs, and sewing the seams.

Lay the boxer shorts at one end of the room with half the members of each team. Put the other half of each team on the opposite side of the room. Give the whole group these instructions:

- On "Go," the first person in each team quickly puts on the shorts, gathering the shorts around her or him as well as possible, runs to the other side of the room, and tags another team member who hops inside the shorts with her or him. The two of them run back to the other side, make room for another team member, and so on. Continue until all the team members have squeezed into the pair of boxer shorts and have run the relay.

(Michael Capps, "Wacky Ways to Form Groups," *Jr. High Ministry*, November–December 1990, p. 32. Reprinted by permission from *Jr. High Ministry* Magazine, copyright © 1993 by Group Publishing, P.O. Box 481, Loveland, CO 80539.)

Sing-Along

Give each small group a piece of paper and a pencil. Offer these directions:

- You will have 3 minutes to write down on your piece of paper the titles of songs of which each member of your small group can sing at least eight words. Write down as many song titles as possible. Once time is called, you will not be allowed to write down any more titles.

    Call time after 3 minutes. Continue with the following directions:

- This is an elimination game. The last small group left with a song to sing wins. When I point to a small group, that group has 3 seconds to begin singing eight words to a song. If other groups have that same song on their list, they must cross it out. There are two ways to be eliminated:

    1. If your group sings a song that has already been sung before.
    2. When you have no more songs to sing.

    Play the game, pointing to various small groups until you have a winner.

Ski Team Relay

Make some skis out of plywood that will accommodate several team members at once. The skis should be approximately four feet long and six inches wide. Use thick plywood that will not break easily. Drill holes in the plywood and put rope through the holes, forming loops for the players' feet. Have each team then race around a goal on these skis.

Staying Put

Give each small group a large piece of newsprint and these instructions:

- Every member of your small group must stand on the newsprint. There may not be any part of anyone's feet hanging over the paper.

    When they have done this successfully, instruct the groups to fold the paper in half and give them the same instructions. Once more, have them fold the newsprint in half and see how many groups can have all their members standing on the paper.

Part B Guided Meditation Tips

- *Read slowly.* Pauses are written into the text for quiet reflection. Do not rush through the text.
- *Read with a little inflection.* A very dramatic reading can be its own distraction. Read beyond a monotone, but try to keep your tone relaxing and conducive to prayer.
- *Read with a rhythm.* After familiarizing yourself with a specific meditation you have chosen, you will recognize its natural rhythm. Flow with that rhythm.
- *Read with confidence.* Before you begin, remind yourself that the Holy Spirit is an active presence. The teens are always in the gentle hands of the Lord during prayer. God will accomplish so much more than any words written or spoken on God's behalf. Be confident in your role as reader and in the role of the Holy Spirit.
- *Find a sacred space.* The location for prayer is often as important as the prayer itself. A sacred environment seems to frame the meditation with an immediate presence of God. Moving to a new location at the outset can create a sense that what follows is different, special, and set aside from everything else. It is important to find an area free from visual distractions. Dimming the lights can also help to create a conducive atmosphere.
- *Listen to the silence.* We are often afraid of silence, hiding from it with radios, televisions, and sound systems. When silence is forced upon us, it is often broken with nervous laughter, whispering, or countless other distractions. Teens are usually uncomfortable at the beginning of the progressive muscle relaxation exercise and then calm down enough to meditate. We usually tell them that we expect some giggling, but that they should try to calm down and enjoy the experience. If any teens are extremely uncomfortable, they may pass, or we may remove them from the room so that they do not distract the others.
- *Use music.* Meditation requires quiet, but soft instrumental music can be used to block unwanted noises and center the teens.
- *Give each person enough space.* Separate the teens as much as possible. We have each teen take his or her own pew or, at most, two teens per pew and have them sit on opposite ends. This not only helps them to get into the meditation but also avoids teens distracting one another.

(Adapted from Catucci, *Time with Jesus,* pp. 10–11)

Part C Muscle Relaxation Exercises

Have the teens sit or lie down in a comfortable position, legs uncrossed and arms at their sides or loose in front of them. Encourage them to close their eyes or stare at something like a candle or piece of stained glass. Remind them that this is not an exercise to get them to fall asleep. Their bodies are at rest, but their minds should be active.

Tense and Relax
- Make a fist with your right hand and tighten the muscles. Then let it go, relax it. Do the same with your other hand. Then make a fist with both hands at the same time. Then relax them.
- Now tighten your whole body. Stretch both arms out, away from your body. Then relax; let your arms flop back down at your sides. Do this a couple of times.
- Shrug your shoulders up high, toward your ears. Then let them drop back down and relax. Do this twice.
- Roll your head around in a circle, slowly. Feel your neck muscles loosen up.
- Press your lips together. Then loosen them.
- Now fill your lungs with air. Breathe in, hold your breath for a few seconds, then breathe out.
- Pull your stomach in. Make it hard and feel your stomach muscles tighten. Now let go and let them relax.
- Arch your back, making it hollow behind you. Then relax.
- Now tighten your leg muscles. First point your toes away from you. Stretch your legs out away from you. Feel the tension in your leg muscles. Then stop pointing and let them relax. Second, bend your feet at the ankles with your toes pointing toward your head. Feel the tight muscles. Now let them relax. Let your feet and your legs relax.
- Take a few more deep breaths without tensing your muscles. Relax for a few moments. How do your muscles feel now? How do you feel?
(Adapted from Youngs, *Stress in Children*, pp. 119–120)

Number Progression
- *Picture the number 1,* . . . and feel your legs relax. . . . Feel the clothing around your legs . . . the shoes on your feet . . . your legs pressed against the floor or seat. . . . As the number 1 begins to fade . . . feel the last bit of tension leave your body by moving from your thighs, . . . down through your knees, . . . your calves, . . . your ankles, . . . and now out the bottom of your feet. . . . Your legs are now completely relaxed. . . .

  Picture the number 2, . . . and feel your arms and hands relax. . . . Feel the clothing around your arms, . . . any jewelry around your wrists or fingers, . . . your arms against the floor or seat. . . . As the number 2 begins to fade . . . feel the last bit of tension leave your body by moving down from your shoulders, . . . through your upper arms, . . . your elbows, . . . your lower arms, . . . your wrists, . . . and now out your fingertips. . . . Your arms are now completely relaxed. . . .

  Picture the number 3, . . . and feel your chest and stomach relax. . . . Be aware of your breathing. . . . Slow your breathing down. . . . Feel your back against the floor or seat. . . . As the number 3 begins to fade . . . feel any weight on your chest begin to rise, . . . making it easier for you to breathe more deeply and slowly. . . . Now your chest and stomach are completely relaxed. . . .

  Picture the number 4, . . . and feel your neck and head relax. . . . Think about and then relax your mouth, . . . your cheekbones, . . . your eyes, . . . your forehead. . . . And as the number 4 begins to fade . . . feel the last bit of stress and tension come up from your neck . . . travel through your lower face, . . . through your eyes, . . . your forehead, . . . and out the top of your head. . . .

Your whole body is now completely relaxed. . . . Take another breath in very slowly and deeply.

Floating on Grace • Slowly close your eyes, . . . and feel the stillness. . . . Become part of the quiet. . . . Enter into the silence . . . and become part of it. . . . Rest . . . peacefully . . . silently. . . .

With your eyes closed . . . drift to a place far away. . . . Drift in your imagination . . . to a large body of water . . . a gentle body of water . . . that laps the shore lazily . . . slowly lapping . . . and lapping . . . the water slowly rising . . . and sliding across the shore . . . then withdrawing . . . and sliding back. . . .

Look at the ripples of the surface . . . moving so slowly . . . so gently. . . . Now slowly take a small step forward. . . . Put your foot into the water. . . . It almost tickles, . . . but there is no sense of it being cold. . . . And it has no feeling of being warm. . . . It's the same temperature as you. . . .

And with another small step . . . you realize that it really isn't water . . . it's thicker . . . and it conforms to you. . . . It seems to hold you up . . . making you feel lighter. . . .

Another step . . . slowly . . . and you're up to your knees. . . . It feels dry . . . and buoyant . . . but it still moves and sparkles like water . . . still lapping near the shore, . . . and there is a great feeling of peace . . . and solitude . . . and comfort . . . comfort.

Take yet another step . . . and another . . . until you're up to your waist. . . . You feel incredibly buoyant . . . almost weight-less . . . like a balloon . . . slowly gliding into the sea. . . .

With great courage . . . you let go . . . slowly lean down . . . and push off . . . as if you would swim. . . . It seems impossible to sink. . . . You feel as if something is holding you up . . . like a bubble. . . .

You roll over on your back . . . look up into blueness. . . . With no effort . . . you float . . . and feel very light . . . almost suspended. . . .

You close your eyes . . . and drift . . . slowly drift . . . as it laps against you so gently. . . . You feel it slowly melting away the pressures, . . . the tensions, . . . the worries. . . . Drifting . . . slowly . . . relaxed, . . . carefree, . . . and weightless.

(Adapted from Catucci, *Time with Jesus,* pp. 23–24)

Part D Tips for Small-Group Facilitators

We have found that junior high students get more out of a retreat if small-group facilitators are enlisted to help. The role of the facilitator is to help the small group carry out the directions that the retreat leader gives them. The following are guidelines for carrying out this role:

- *Affirm.* Give each teenager genuine compliments when possible.
- *Guide.* When behavior is inappropriate, remind the group of any retreat standards that have been explained and posted at the beginning of the retreat. The following are common retreat standards:
  - What's said here, stays here.
  - Only one person speaks at a time.
  - Put-downs, both verbal and physical, are off-limits.
  - Questions are welcomed.
  - You may decline when invited to share.
  - Be open and try.
- *Encourage.* Try to involve all teenagers in every activity.
- *Respect.* Treat the comments and opinions of all teenagers equally.
- *Share.* See yourself as a member of the group, and do not dominate.
- *Listen.* Make sure everyone has a chance to speak. Show through your body language and verbal comments that the speaker has been heard.
- *Question.* Use questions and comments such as these: "What do the rest of you think?" or "Good comment. Who has something to add?" If a teenager says something off the wall, instead of rejecting the comment, say: "That's not exactly what I expected. Would you like to try again?"

Acknowledgments *(continued)*

The statistic on page 7 is from an article by David Balsiger, *Group* Magazine, February 1995, page 16.

The Survival Game on pages 32–33 and the material on handout 2–C are adapted from *Twenty New Ways of Teaching the Bible,* by Donald L. Griggs (Nashville: Abingdon Press, 1979), page 27. Copyright © 1977 by Griggs Educational Service. Used with permission.

Loneliness Easers on pages 34–35, the material on handout 2–F, and Sex Media Search on pages 101–102 are adapted by permission from *Jr. High Retreats and Lock-Ins,* by Karen Dockrey (Loveland, CO: Group Books, 1990), pages 161–162, 163, and 93–95, respectively. Copyright © 1990 by Karen Dockrey. Published by Group Publishing, P.O. Box 481, Loveland, CO 80539.

Givens and Changeables on pages 51–52, The Factory on pages 55–56, and World Simulation Game on pages 57–59 are adapted from *Rich World, Poor World: A Curriculum Resource on Youth and Development,* by Alyson Huntly (Dubuque, IA: Willliam C. Brown, 1987), pages 277–278; 175, 185; and 67–70, respectively. Copyright © 1987 by Brown-ROA, a division of Harcourt Brace and Company. Used by permission of the publisher.

But I Say to You on pages 53–54 and the material on handout 3–A are adapted from *Poverty: Do It Justice!* edited by Thomas Bright (New Rochelle, NY: Don Bosco Multimedia, 1993), pages 89 and 90. Copyright © 1993 by Center for Ministry Development. Used with permission.

Gilbert and the Color Orange on pages 54–55 is adapted from *Teaching Peace,* by Ruth Fletcher (New York: Harper and Row, 1987), pages 29–30. Copyright © 1987 by Ruth Fletcher. Used by permission of HarperCollins Publishers.

Different Tastes on pages 70–71 is adapted by permission from *Group's Active Bible Curriculum: Today's Music: Good or Bad?* edited by Stephen Parolini (Loveland, CO: Group Publishing, 1990), pages 27–28. Copyright © 1990 by Group Publishing, P.O. Box 481, Loveland, CO 80539.

Name Affirmation on page 74, Back to Back on page 111, Bob! Bob! Bob! on page 111, Line Up on page 112, Shuffle the Deck on page 113, Body Balloon Burst on page 115, and Knots on pages 115–116 are from *Up Close and Personal: How to Build Community in Your Youth Group,* by Wayne Rice (El Cajon, CA: Youth Specialties, 1989), pages 71, 32, 34, 67, 83, 34, and 64–65, respectively. Copyright © 1989 by Youth Specialties, 1224 Greenfield Drive, El Cajon, CA 92091. Used by permission.

The story about Wilma Rudolph on pages 83–84 is adapted from "The Dream of Winning," in *Learning the Skills of Peacemaking,* revised and expanded edition, by Naomi Drew (Rolling Hills Estates, CA: Jalmar Press, 1995), page 138. Copyright © 1995 by Jalmar Press. Used by permission of Jalmar Press.

Today's Teens on pages 95–97 and What's New? on pages 98–100 are adapted by permission from *Group's Active Bible Curriculum: Guys and Girls: Understanding Each Other,* edited by Michael D. Warden (Loveland, CO: Group Publishing, 1991), pages 14–15 and 24–26. Copyright © 1991 by Group Publishing, P.O. Box 481, Loveland, CO 80539.

Group Up on page 112 and Kooky Kickball on page 116 are adapted from *Play It! Over Four Hundred Great Games for Groups,* by Wayne Rice and Mike Yaconelli (Grand Rapids, MI: Zondervan Publishing House, 1986), pages 146 and 29. Copyright © 1986 by Youth Specialties. Used by permission of Zondervan Publishing House.

Lap Game on page 112 is adapted from *New Games for the Whole Family,* by Dale N. LeFevre (New York: Perigee Books, 1988), page 131. Copyright © 1988 by Dale N. LeFevre. Used with permission of the Berkley Publishing Group. All rights reserved.

Backward Letter Scramble on page 114 is adapted from *Creative Activities for Small Youth Groups,* compiled by Wayne Rice and Mike Yaconelli (Winona, MN: Saint Mary's Press, 1991), pages 81–82. Copyright © 1991 by Youth Specialties, 1224 Greenfield Drive, El Cajon, CA 92021. Used by permission.

Connect-a-Name on page 115 is adapted from *Play It Again! More Great Games for Groups,* by Wayne Rice and Mike Yaconelli (Grand Rapids, MI: Zondervan Publishing House, 1993), page 168. Copyright © 1993 by Youth Specialties. Used by permission of Zondervan Publishing House.

The guided meditation tips on page 119 and the muscle relaxation exercise Floating on Grace on page 121 are adapted from *Time with Jesus: Twenty Guided Meditations for Youth,* by Thomas F. Catucci (Notre Dame, IN: Ave Maria Press, 1993), pages 10–11 and 23–24. Copyright © 1993 by Ave Maria Press, Notre Dame, IN 46556. Used by permission of the publisher.

The muscle relaxation exercise Tense and Relax on page 120 is adapted from *Stress in Children: How to Recognize, Avoid, and Overcome It,* by Dr. Bettie B. Youngs (New York: Arbor House, 1985), pages 119–120. Copyright © 1985 by Arbor House.